ENTERING THE GROVE

ENTERING *The* GROVE

Photography
Gary Braasch
Text
Kim R. Stafford

PEREGRINE SMITH BOOKS

SALT LAKE CITY

The authors and publisher are contributing to
tree planting and preservation programs. We urge
you to do the same. See the list of actions to
take, "Plant A Thousand Trees," at the end of this
book.

This is a Peregrine Smith Book, published by
Gibbs Smith, Publisher
P.O. Box 667, Layton, UT 84041
Book design by Principia Graphica, Portland, OR
Cover photographs: *Hemlock Forest* and *Western
White Pine Log* by Gary Braasch

Printed and bound in Hong Kong by Everbest
95 94 93 92 91 90   8 7 6 5 4 3 2 1

Library of Congress Cataloging-in-Publication Data
Stafford, Kim Robert.
    Entering the grove / Kim Stafford ; with
photographs by Gary Braasch.
    p.   c.m.
    ISBN 0-87905-302-X
    1. Stafford, Kim Robert—Biography. 2. Authors,
American—20th century—Biography. 3. Trees.
I. Braasch, Gary. II. Title.
PS3569.T23Z464 1990
818'.5403-dc20   90-7200
[B]   CIP

Text printed on recycled paper

Like the trees, we are visitors, guests of earth. The light shines down, and a bud breaks, branches give way before us, a book's leaves open, and our eyes look, look again. We are a grove, companions spared to be on earth at the same time. The trees—though not our kind—are kin, elder relatives standing to greet us.

Kim Stafford, from Tree of All Trees

Contents

Also by Kim Stafford:

Having Everything Right

Places & Stories

The Granary

A Gypsy's History of the World

Also by Gary Braasch:

The Northwest, Pacific Coast and Cascades

Secrets of the Old Growth Forest

Photographing the Patterns of Nature

ENTERING THE GROVE

COSTA RICA

FIR AND HEMLOCK FOREST

COSTA RICA

BIRCH

COLUMBIA RIVER GORGE

BIRCH AND DOGWOOD

ALDERS

WESTERN RED CEDAR

ALDERS

NEW HAMPSHIRE

COSTA RICA

YELLOWSTONE RIVER CANYON

The Tree of All Trees

One morning in the city I began to learn from trees. Tangled in my love's arms, I woke from the dream that showed me the Tree of All Trees, one great shape looming up, its red bark braided with silver and brown. Its trunk towered over the earth, reaching out one cedar limb, a limb of cherry, a twig white with honey locust, a pear branch humming with bees. The tree's fist held willow that swayed, a twitching hazel bush. From that trunk, apple boughs bent with fruit, and an ashwood stem divided the light. Every bird dwelt in the tree's green dome, blue wing and red, singing. Hail scoured one side while sun lit the other. Buds opened, petals shook loose, and the wind sang through.

Outside the house, snow moaned past the window. A blizzard had come up in the night. I lay still, held my love sleeping, or perhaps she was awake, waiting. Soon we would speak. But not yet. By first light I could see the outline a maple made through the slats of venetian blind. Winter held the world, but something there inside, at the center, breathed life with me.

That tree from my dream invited me to enter the grove of the world, to put my fingers against each trunk and feel the pitchy braid of its bark. Trees are guardians of the Earth, and we are the guardians of trees. We rely on what we know of them, how well we see their dominion over the planet. They spin our breath into being, giving it in little sips. They scatter shade and literally hold the mountains together with their roots. When we are lost, they heal our misery. What is human history but a long conversation between the old urge of the green leaf and the hunger of our stone, bronze, or steel blade? There is a cunning in the crooked teeth of a saw, a cunning pertinent to our daily lives. There is also a life surge in old trees that is key to our long survival.

I climb into my life from that dream, just as trees keep climbing into shapes printed in the seed. From my bedroom, I look to the mountains. I want to ramble the forest where the natural world works wild and right. I want to be loyal to the ways of earth, living by grit and wind, surviving fire and flood, relishing a mayhem of green. Out there, when spring comes and the light shines full, a leaf flame will bloom. A root strikes through schist. In the forest, trees brave seasons of drought and apples, of nut hull and bare snag, geotropic root punching out the acorn, sapling at the solstice rushing into its fullest being. Lightning strikes, or fire holds back for a thousand years. It's not just in my dream. In my front yard, along the street, along the road to the mountains, trees hold greater authority than stone to flex and heal. I see their amazing grace and power to seek light, to split concrete for a sip of water, to bud at the timberline after a scouring by winter ice, to disobey when rock says no. Everywhere I look trees plunge into earth, climb the sky, sip fog from the wind and swallow iron from the earth. They are not patient but present, in place, accountable to the moment. Cedar speaks a green word. I can smell it. Oak on a hilltop shrugs off centuries. In its shade, I waken again to the bristling Tree of All Trees, the vivid neighborhood of the world.

In the forest, I want to remember stories that hold the flavor of the grove, stories that summon the whisper and chill of single trees and whole hillsides, watersheds, islands, continents. I want to inhabit these stories by telling them to you. I want memory to be the quiet voice over my shoulder while I look on bark, and leaf, and blossom. In the forest, I find myself moving from story to story, stepping through the grove like a series of pools, each story inhabiting a hollow of sand, turning there until a thread of water links forward to the next.

Each tree stands as time made visible, years made fragrant. Somewhere near, the yew tree bows down, guarding an anonymous place. When you walk under or climb its limbs, you may taste the sticky flavor of the yew's own life. Its breath of pitch and pollen becomes your breath. Put your head against the red trunk. Lean hard enough to know wood with your skull, though skin and bark keep busy between you.

I want to summon the trees of our home because nothing lives alone. We are a grove on Earth, serving one another. Pablo Neruda said, "I would do for you what spring does for the cherry trees." That force blooms like laughter. By it we inhabit the world. Like the trees, we are visitors, guests of earth. The light shines down, and a bud breaks, branches give way before us, a book's leaves open, and our eyes look, look again. We are a grove, companions spared to be on earth at the same time. The trees—though not our kind—are kin, elder relatives standing to greet us.

When I step from the house at dawn, into blizzard or blossom time, the trees beckon me to enter the grove. The grove is a single tree, or it is the wilderness unfurled across the mountains. In bed with my love, I dreamed of the tree of all trees. Now I set out to seek it.

The Ravens

Wherever you are, I want to say to you here at the beginning, "Look again." Memory works by looking again, as do science, and forgiveness. I have learned this by being wrong, being changed. I have learned to slow down to zero, and study what's in front of my face. A tree spirals around as it grows. I turn and look again. I will tell you how the ravens taught me to look again.

Out in the Wallowa Mountains of Oregon, I lay down for sleep near Joseph Canyon. I had been teaching in Idaho, and my teaching had been a failure. It is hard to fail at what you call yourself. I rolled out my thin summer sleeping bag on the needle duff in a gathering of young pines. I had left the lights of Lewiston far behind, the constellations of house and street scattered over the hills. I had driven the contortions of the road over the Grande Ronde River and up, past the last farm light and on. I smoothed the ground and slid into the bag. At the dark rim of Joseph Canyon, the city is all in the stars, lit and turning bright as the earliest time. A whisper in the trees, and sleep came thick.

In the morning, two shouting ravens woke me, leering from the branch where they swayed. When I stood, they flapped about clumsily, circling my head, then flying away to the east, fanning their wings to a stall, and settling on the meadow. When I followed, stepped close, they leaped up to circle my head again, with their rusty croak and wing whisk. The rainbow black of their feathers held all color in a sheen where they flashed about me. Then they went east a way, settled again, hopped, pivoted, cocked their heads, and waited for me. I followed. They flew and settled. I followed. And at last we came to the canyon rim, where the slope dropped away to blue distance. This time they jumped, hunched their wings about me in the air a last time, coughed so their throat feathers shook, and then they flew straight away east without a backward glance. They sailed away over the tall hump of the canyon air, dwindling until they were lost against the dark ridgeline of the Seven Devils in Idaho.

I sat down at the rim, feeling I had been summoned, and would be taught something. I felt I might see an eagle or a bear by the ravens' beckoning. Surely something great with purpose would rise before me. The canyon unrolled an endless journey for the eyes at that place, shoulders of meadow and rock angling down with ribbons of trees between them. Great loops of wind swung through the pines, and the crimson glint of the flowers called Indian paintbrush flickered on the grassy slope below me. Serviceberry bushes flashed their buttons of green, and sage softened the hillside gray. Tiny vagabond spiders rode their web filaments adrift in the updraft.

I gazed a long time. A buzzard drifted north. My shadow moved. A butterfly flickered bright before me. The pines grew still. Then the heat shimmered toward noon. Nothing. No message I could see. The stones got harder under me, the headache sun climbed as it beat on my head. And I stood up, hobbled awhile, then walked limp and faint back the way I had come.

Grasshoppers shattered thick from the grass. They rattled from every bush, bounced from stones gray with lichens. A fat spider hung like a rosehip from a twig, hung nibbling on a grasshopper furled in its web, twirling it round. When I crouched to watch it, the spider did not flinch. The whole bush hummed with life: ants working twig and leaf, hunting any sparkle of dew before the sun hissed it away. I thought I could hear their small feet rattle on the wood. Here and there a spiderweb hung ravaged by the night traffic of small wings.

Then, to my left in the bush, I saw this at a twig tip: two creatures locked into one knot, another grasshopper being eaten by this hunching shape clamped to it. But this time the victim had open eyes. It was purple, wet, studying me as its life dwindled. So, the end.

But then I looked again. No, the darker shape was a grasshopper too. The two were locked together loving, tangled into one being making more, making next year's meadow twinkle and sing. A leaf twitched and the twig shook. Yes, the beginning.

Then I looked yet again. Not death. Not lover. The darker shape was simply a husk, the old shell split open along the back where the grasshopper had climbed out of itself. Something spun me into place. Something hammered me. Over my shoulder came stories that shook me. I loved my brother, but he died. The love I felt for a woman died. I climbed out from the husk of those days. Pain did not explain it. No one could explain it. And here hunched the grasshopper, living through change. The soft, purple being I took for victim, and then companion, was simply new. Resting. Vulnerable. Bright in the eye.

I stood up, staggered. Swaying like a pine, I thought back. The ravens do not teach by saying, "Look at this," pointing with a wingtip, poking the beak at it. They prefer to lead their student among the secrets woven into the whole fabric of the place. They say, "Come over this way, and have a look around. Maybe you will see."

If I have failed, if we have failed the Earth, we may turn to it again. Some of us may act the raven.

A Woman Named Tree

Over and over, I learn to look again. What would my life be like if I did not have a daughter named Rosemary and a friend named Tree? When my daughter and I crouch inside the hollow room of a cedar tree, she sees what I don't yet see.

"Dad, these trees never die. Something gives them light." The sunlight brightens, and she looks out by the crack we entered, into the swaying spangle of the forest.

"Dad, let's say you are a bear, and this is your home. Let's pretend we are both bears, and we were just born." And we step out into the grove. We step like moss, like cubs, like fog. She shouts, and a cedar seed comes spinning past her hands.

Back in the city, she keeps teaching me. The apple tree in the front yard is too slender for Rosemary to climb, but she climbs it anyway. I see it as a thin young apple tree; she sees more as her imagination climbs.

"I always wanted a dad like you!" she shouts from the tree. "I dreamed about it when I was little!" She has taken her blanket and pillow into the spindly limbs.

One morning she rubs her eyes and tells her dream:

"A monster man was chasing us," she says, "cutting off everyone's heads. They waited in line, and he killed them. But when it was our turn, we ran to the apple tree, and climbed it. The branches started waving like wind, but they turned into wings, and the tree carried us into the sky, and inside the tree was a little room with beds, and food and drinks, and then we put casts on all the people's necks, and they were alive, and I woke up."

She knows about belonging. I put my hand on the trunk of the little apple tree in the yard, on the wrist at its slender fork. It is stronger than it looks. Her tree will be stronger as she grows. And what of your tree? All my stories are about where you live, about the tree in your yard, the battered elm that shades you as you walk your street, the sumac volunteer climbing the slope by the culvert, your hilltop oak. You know the tree I mean. When you stand beside it, and look beyond, you will belong. John Muir found between every two pines a doorway to a new world. Stepping through that door, he was a wild, free man. At your own tree, your private grove, your doorway to the forest world, this belonging begins.

If we look again at the language we use daily, we will see how deep this belonging goes. My daughter favors trees, and my oldest neighbors grow toward the grace of old trees, because they both share a longing for the deepest truth of being. A tree can comfort them as no word of mine. Somehow, the oldest and youngest among us seem to live at the heartwood of life.

I know this as a father, and as a son. And this deepens what I know as a scholar, that a thousand years ago the English words for "tree" and "true" were a single word. We spelled both the green creature and the honored quality *treow*. Over the centuries, that word branched to two, sprouted a thicket of cousins from "durable" to "truce," and evolved through a multitude of forms.

What could be more alive yet reliable than a tree, more stable, unyielding? I am talking about an old tree, one that was here before the most distant grandparents we know. The definitions of "true" are all about trees, for trees are steadfast, firm in allegiance, constant. They are reliable, honest, upright, unfeigned. They live consistent with fact. They represent the thing as it is. They are accurately placed, exact in position. A tree stands true to the ancestral type. A tree keeps its promises, pays its debt to the place it lives. How can I be this honest?

Once, in a crowded lobby, a fine old woman named Eve snatched my hand, read my palm in a glance, and silenced the company with her shout, "You are a good lover, but not a great one!" I felt my face heat up, and my friends all studied me, smiling. But Eve ignored them all. "Ah," she said to my eyes, "when I was young, far from home, I was so slain by loneliness I went to the Grove of the Professors, threw my arms about an oak, and wept. The bark against my cheek was wet, and I held tight and shook. All the world seemed to conspire against me, and I was small." Her hand tightened on my wrist. Her eyes softened. "But then a voice from the grove said to me, 'Shun those who love you not—in spite of your faults,' and I was comforted. I was healed into myself." She released my hand. We all stood still, and Eve drifted away through the grove we made.

I trace my roots, and tell my child the family tree. There is one page in my Bible that bears my grandmother's hand, writing the names and years of our people. Where my finger traces, that tree holds them all. But that tree is bigger than my family's names. To be true, like a seed drifting downwind, I turn from the family to my friends.

I have a wise friend named Tree, a maker of fine books, a designer learning form from the calligraphic swirl of water, the way the horizon line kinks and climbs for mountains, the true shapes of trunks and limbs. Some days her custom is to stand for long periods quite still, lifting her body in the breathless configuration of a letter—T, for example, upright, poised, with her arms stretched flat and her head tilted out of the way. She thinks about T, and the tree. The world goes away then, leaves Tree alone. Her mind is still and her arms are strong. Like cedar. Like yew, the living talisman of change. Then the tree steps away from her, like a shadow with an independent frame of mind. She stirs, exits from her meditation and returns to work.

One day at the coast, I saw a freak white-winged crow courted by an all-black crow. They preened and gabbled on the rain-lit meadow. I looked uphill at forest and fog. At my back the ocean hushed. The white-winged crow, fluttering and hopping on the earth, faced her companion and stood her ground, while her suitor strutted round and round. When his circle tightened, she flew into a short pine, and he sprang up to banter and flap in the limbs below her. She stood up somehow taller than her body. The shoulders of her wings lifted and swaggered. Her eye flashed. The pine shook. Rain fell.

"Tree!" I called, "Tree, come and look." It felt right to call out that word, and she came. Tree stood beside me and we gazed at those two birds settled now, a mated diversity, aloof and calm, resting in the pine.

When the green world flickers, some event roots the traveler long enough to see.

The World Tree Named Yggdrasil

The forest is a library where fire might come, where roads penetrate and trucks cart off the centuries in thirty-two-foot lengths. A little man may kill a great tree. But for a long time we have made stories about the World Tree, the great trunk that will survive us all. Somehow the power of stars gets grafted to the seed, and the seed buds tall. In its dimension, in the realm of dream and in the mythic fact of whole forests, the rust of generations may nibble axes to nothing, while the World Tree grows.

An Old English manuscript called The Vercelli Book holds one such story. Some monk traveling from the island of England must have carried this manuscript to Italy soon after the tenth century, and left it in the Cathedral at Vercelli, in Italy, where no one read it for centuries. Old books share this with the heartwood of old trees: a fragrant secret about time. On three leaves deep in the book a poem tells a dream about a tree, how that tree spoke a jeweled explosion of sounds, a visionary shimmer of syllables. Let me translate, as I can, the beginning.

"*Hwaet!*" it cries, "Listen, I will tell the choicest dream that came to me in the middle of the night, after the bearers of speech lay down to rest. It seemed to me I saw the best tree lifted into the air, tailored with light, the brightest beam. All that beacon was wrapped in gold; gems stood where the tree reached to the corners of the Earth. . . ."

Gradually, reading, I see that the tree speaking is the Cross, about to tell the story of its making, how it was hewn, and used in the crucifixion. But this old poem does more. It tells of the Cross of Christianity, but it also crosses over to older pagan imagery. Hovering in the sky, grasping the corners of the world, this tree summons the Norse tree *Yggdrasil,* the great ash tree that stood as spine to the world, dripping dew like honey that drew the bees. In the old Norse cosmology, the tree Yggdrasil cast roots into Hell, budded in Heaven, and spread its shimmer of limbs and leaves far over the fields and forests of Middle Earth. Yggdrasil rooted at the center before the world began, and will survive Ragnarok, the volcanic end of the world in ice and fire. It is what folklorists call the World Tree, or the Guardian Tree, one trunk that props a ladder between worlds, that sustains and nourishes all creatures, even as the world's hungry multitude nibbles at its roots and twigs.

According to the *Voluspa,* the great collection of Norse mythology from ca. A.D. 1000, this great tree is at the hinge of change from time to eternity. When the last three winters have frozen the Earth but before the fire comes, two people will take shelter in this tree, a man and a woman, Lif and Lifthrasir, feeding on its dew, safe in Yggdrasil. The Earth will writhe and grow dark, but within the tree, they two will not be touched. The gods will fight and fall. Everyone will be gone, everything outside the tree will be destroyed. They two will huddle together within, and the tree, scorched but massive with life, will guard them. Then, through the first new leaves they will see light return. They will emerge, kindle life, bear children, and the new world will begin.

In the Old English poem, all this pagan story plays undertone to the tree's own voice. The dream is charged with a sturdy heartwood voice from long before, from the older Druidic worship of trees. Reading, I taste pollen and rain, feel the tongue's buzz, overhear a sweet chant from the old world. The poem says, "that best wood spoke a word." Then the tree begins, "It was very long ago—I yet remember it—that I was hewn at the grove's edge, struck from my root." The tree tells a tough, heroic story of a young hero climbing, and dark nails driven, and blood, and how the weight of the world grew heavy, and all creation wept.

I do believe a tree's first words would be, "It was very long ago—I yet remember it." Time in the tree billows as a concentric moment, unfurling in place, an urgency of pitch and leaf, tireless as a folktale: One time before all time, when there was no season or word, when the stars forgot to dim at dawn, and the meadows held their dew as the sun climbed, then tiny seeds swallowed great vines into themselves and leaped into pods that dwindled older and began. The world began and wind carried its story. Leaf by leaf the years unfurled. Fire might come, or some tiny man with an ax, so the green world grows.

The Peg at the Heart of Play

Lay your hand on a table. A warmth rises to greet you, for wood lives when the tree dies. Physicists are learning this, and musicians have known for a long time. There was once a physicist who also played the violin. One morning, he took his fiddle to the lab, wrapped it green with felt, clamped it gently in a vise, and trained the electron microscope close on the spruce belly, just beside the f-hole, where a steel peg was set humming at a high frequency. Through the microscope, once he got it honed in right, he saw the molecular surface of the wood begin to pucker and ripple outward like rings on a pond, the ripples rising gradually into waves, and the peg a blur at the heart of play.

When he drew the peg away, the ripples did not stop. In twenty-four hours, the ripples had not stopped. He saw, still, a concentric tremor on the molecular quilt of the wood. The violin, in the hard embrace of the vise, had a thing to say, a song. But then, in another twelve hours, the ripple had flattened and the wood lay inert.

Musicians know this without a microscope. A wooden instrument of ebony, maple, and spruce suffers a small death if not played daily. Cut thin, spruce revels in its responsive hum. A guitar, a violin, or a lute chills the air for the first ten minutes of fresh play. It will need to be quickened from scratch. But the fiddle played every day hangs resonant on the wall, quietly boisterous when it first is lifted down, already trembling, anxious to speak, to cry out, to sing at the bow's first stroke. Not to rasp, but to sing. The instrument is in tune before the strings are tuned.

I like to think of standing trees thrumming inwardly after a storm has played them hard, or humming quietly after the breeze has brushed their slender height. The forest does not live intermittently, and we do not. Our hopes practice a resonant blur. I learned this from an old musician who used to say: If I don't practice for even one day, I can tell the difference when I next cradle the cello in my arms. If I fail to practice for two days, my close friends can also tell the difference. If I don't practice three days, the whole world knows.

His words teach me about my own life, how I feel as I write about trees. Places and stories beckon, and I comply, building a mosaic of stories. Each story is a peg that startles my life into being. I want to tell about the nun who lived as a tree in her room at the convent, rooted in place, she said, but buffeted by all the emotions one can feel, shaken like a willow in the storm.

And I remember Forest Francisco, my old friend who planted his yard with Douglas fir seedlings at the age of eighty-eight, planted them close so they would grow straight until they were old. He knelt in the dew and showed me. "See how close I put them?" he said. "They gotta be close to grow straight, straight and tall by the time they're old." When he was young, he had dug out thirteen old-growth stumps by hand. Yet in old age he wanted them to grow again, to bury the sunlight he had wrested from the forest. I had to help him up. He staggered on my arm. We laughed about it.

I want to tell about my old teacher, at the end, how he asked to have his ashes scattered under the pines; about my friends who have named their newborn son Cedar. When pain or exhilaration shakes me, I feel a chlorophyllic buzz of life. Telling stories, shaping words daily on the page, with the first stroke my hand may swim, the pen glide. My pen is the peg that would move the hearts of those I love.

What resonates in your life? Where do you feel your own rush? Where is the tree that starts your understanding? Somewhere near you stands an oldest tree. No matter how old it is, it is oldest in that place, and it reigns quietly in the neighborhood. I think of the hemlock I used to camp beside, down in the woods near my house. It had the shaggy look of something there before any of us. I would build a small fire in the clay beside it, and wait for dusk, the time when silence included me. It was my older but indulgent cousin. The biggest tree, the oldest one, stands near you somewhere yet. I ask my friends where this monarch dwells. "Oh yes," says Dana in Oregon, "that would be the maple I played in as a child. We had a room in the low branches, and there was the saddle limb for reading. Then I was married under that tree—it is really two grown together—and at the end of the ceremony we simply stood awhile silent and let the green light fall over us."

"Yes," says Ken from Maine, "my favorite toy was a particular elm. As a child I pitied my friends when they bragged about their toys. They had fine things, but I had that tree. And my favorite game was simply to watch the coins of sunlight flicker across my hands. Did that for hours."

"Oldest?" says an old California native in the Silicon Valley. "Just go down where those freeways cross in Mountain View. Down under there is an oak that's oldest. You have to scramble off the overpass and push through the scotch broom. Got bees in it. Poison oak. Lots of litter. Old tires and thistle. Doing fine, though, last time I checked."

"Our tree," says Cecelia from Alaska, "is a little scrubby spruce not knee-high that somehow keeps alive out there on the tundra. People put up a sign beside it: 'Welcome to the Bethel National Forest.' Just that one tree. Snow covers it, then there it is again green. It's our little joke we're fond of."

West from Los Angeles, it's the oak that leans to scatter acorns. In Junction City, Kansas, it's the elm on the hilltop lightning favors. In San Antonio, Texas, it's the pepper tree spreading inside the compound at the Alamo. In the Smokies of Carolina, it's the tree my friend calls Heart Bursting Open. West from Bloomfield, Connecticut, it's the sycamore the centuries left alone, so massive the whole world suddenly shrinks to a different scale. To guard the whole earth, it is necessary to be large, or many, or old, or profoundly nourishing, or all of these. I put my ear against a maple in the storm to hear that symphonic rattle of twigs. My ear is wet and my heart jumps.

When I am in the forest in a storm, I feel the world thrum as one great violin. I am the peg that walks.

ALDERS

BIRCH

RED OSIER DOGWOOD

DOGWOOD AND SNOWBERRY

PINE AND MAPLES

VINE MAPLES AND ALDERS

COLUMBIA RIVER GORGE

OAK AND BIRCH

VINE MAPLES AND ALDERS

MAPLES AND DOGWOOD

BASALT AND ALDERS

GREAT SMOKY MOUNTAINS

MOJAVE DESERT

Crossing to Long Island: Brooklyn

Kuo Hsi, the eleventh-century Sung painter, said "there are land-scapes one can walk through, landscapes which can be gazed upon, landscapes in which one may ramble, and landscapes in which one may dwell." After studying many mountains, many land-scapes, he concluded that "those fit for walking through or being gazed upon are not equal to those in which one may ramble or one may dwell." He wanted wilderness to be portable through art. He wanted us to be forest hermits at court, or hermits in the throng and noise of the city, by unfolding a screen of mountain scenery brushed on silk. "How delightful," he said, "to have a land-scape painting rendered by some skillful hand! Without leaving the room, a person may find himself sitting among streams and ravines; the cries of monkeys and birds faintly reach his ears, light on the hills and reflection on the water, glittering, dazzle his eyes."

The thing most necessary for viewing art and find-ing peace, according to Kuo, is to hold within yourself "the heart of forests and streams," not only to be in the forest, but to have the forest in you. A way of seeing, not just the thing seen, brings delight. The green world surges into the welcoming mind.

How can I invite the heart of mountains and streams into myself? How can I carry the forest into the city? I know from my own life this is a matter of survival, not aesthetics. Concrete kills. Little by little, sirens gnaw at the mind. At the pit of long-ing, there is nothing so cruel as a phone that will not ring. I live in the city, but the city does not give me life. Trees give me life.

Once, sitting alone by the elm-shrouded library, at the dizzy-minded end of a long day, I wanted to smuggle the forest into the city. I wanted the hemlocks to march, to throng my city's canyons. I wanted the alders to line that street named for them. Hobos call my city of Portland, Oregon, "Stumptown." The name is an elegy. Maybe the nickname of every city is a kind of elegy to what was there before. But what about the Big Apple? The taller the skyscrapers the deeper the shade. If I set out from Wall Street, how far would I need to walk to enter the green world? To Central Park? Too tame. To that ragged hillside at The Cloisters? A fragment. What about Long Island? What if I walked from the heart of the city, over the bridge to Long Island, looking for a wilderness? What if I walked over the bridge into Brooklyn, seek-ing something older than brick? Walking, I would hold the heart of forests and streams. I would look again.

If a tree grows in Brooklyn still, perhaps it is Yggdrasil, the resident oldest one. But friends advised me to dream of more beautiful places. Long Island was once lovely, they said, but these days I could do better—flee to Maine, say, or take up the Adirondack Trail, climb up from Vermont roads into the mountains. If I did insist on Long Island itself, they said, I ought to visit Cold Springs Harbor, or Nissequogue, or the historic wonder of Levittown, the peculiar customs of Babylon, the eastering run of the Sunrise Highway. I might work my way along the points and bays of Long Island Sound, or venture clear out east to Camp Hero and Montauk. "Stand there at the lighthouse," they said, "in a hurricane."

Something made me stubborn. At Grand Central Station, I studied the limousine route-list for Long Island: Roslyn, Westbury, Hicksville, Plainview, Melville, Brentwood, Hauppauge, Ronkonkoma, Medford, Brookhaven, Riverhead. That sounded exotic, but my plan was more humble. My ambition was not so much for distance. I meant to venture onto Long Island under my own power, to walk east into Brooklyn. "Brooklyn!" said my friends. "That's not the real Long Island at all." But it was my purpose to travel in small ways and learn a little at eye level, sauntering at the pace my slow mind works.

I rambled up onto the wood pedestrian deck of the Brooklyn Bridge one snowy January evening, to spend a night having a look around in the streets at the far west tip of Long Island. If trees could live there, I could live. The place, even with snow and a bitter wind, had invited me.

"Keep moving," a friend told me as I set out from Soho, "and carry a stick. If you curl up to sleep someplace, you're likely to wake up dead." As I paused on the bridge and turned away from the wind, this advice reminded me of my summer in Alaska. There, as I set off through the willows the big bears haunt, I was advised, "Ring a bell, or sing out loud all the way. You surprise a big brown in there, you're gone." In Alaska, I rang the bell the first ten minutes of bushwhacking, sang for a mile, then took mercy on the place and thrashed north in silence. It was the mosquitoes that nearly finished me, where I stood in the damp smoke of a willow fire that wavered. I found the big tracks of bear, laid my watch in the toe of one, peeked constantly over my shoulders like a wary bird. The whining flocks of mosquitoes nudged me to the edge of madness. The bears left me be.

In Brooklyn, as in Alaska, I wanted to see at eye level, to probe with my feet along the track of the wild. Dark made a mapped place wild. I wanted to look obliquely upon the settled customs of an old place, to be alone, vulnerable to it, hospitable to the risks of knowing. At the same time, I was truly afraid. This wasn't my territory. Here, the wildlife carried knives. The carnivores had tattoos. And it was January. On a very cold night, thought can crystallize.

Down off the bridge ramp, I read a shredded poem glued to a lamppost of aluminum. Someone's parody of the Frost poem began, "Whose head this was, I think I know. . . ." Someone had fashioned a vision of war from Frost's "Whose woods these are. . . ." Whose head, whose woods? I rambled south and west into Brooklyn Heights, rambled through salted slush, clubbed my feet against the curb to warm them, mingled with the evening rush-hour walking crowd, stood on a corner in my vagabond coat until the wind urged me on. Where were the trees? I saw them glimmering here and there, sycamores with their little seed balls swinging, and other trunks blurred by snow.

My feet were cold. Burrowing like a mole, I went down the stairway into the subway. There I sat warm with the ragged inhabitants of the Clark Street Station as they mended the knees and elbows of their clothes, bantered, shuffled their debris, and prepared for the long night. A woman was building a quilt of emerald polyester scrap, and chattering stories and demands. After a shudder below us, doors lurched open and subway travelers spun through the turnstiles like a waterfall climbing. Then it was very still. I felt like a character in a story that had not begun. After a time, I climbed to the street, rambled again, the out-of-town guest at the party, who knows no one, the mammal in the grove without a nest.

A stranger in the gloom, I felt like an archeologist of the living, a botanist after the volcano. I studied the flat pigeon fossilized by ice at the end of Pineapple Lane, savored the soft and watery warmth from a steam grate, glimpsed the faces of cabbies lit by TV light where they waited in a narrow room for calls. I stood vigil beside an eviction heap of earthly goods tossed down the steps from a rooming house (shirts, lamp, three shoes, slacks, toaster, spoon, a scatter of rice). I wanted the story of that tenant's life, but only these things remained, a heap under a sidewalk tree. I put my hand on the wet trunk, a skin of ice.

In a diner I feasted on a baked potato heavily laced with pepper for warmth, then hugged a coffee cup. I reviewed the night. Dark had thickened as the hours grew small. I had passed tree-of-heaven saplings writhing out from cracks beside buildings, weaving wood through every chain-link fence, bristling up through a shopping cart abandoned on its side, punching out from the ground with a kind of ecstatic thrust. My friend called it the ghetto tree. Where the pavement cracked, weeds surged into the neighborhood, a generous invasion, a forgiveness. My coffee was done. No one offered me more. I hunched with my elbows set on the twin worn spots in formica. On the wall poster, a few twisted trees decorated a Greek island.

Outside, I walked an alley, came out near Willow Street. Standing in the snow, my feet starting to numb, I watched my summer memory bloom against a blank brick wall. In August, I had rambled up Flatbush Avenue to the Brooklyn Botanical Garden, those blocks where leaves billowed over walls in an impossible generosity of living shade. Now, the wall where I stood in snow softened, and trees loomed into my head. Memory took me again to the garden, where great trees leaned over the walls to shade the sidewalk, a forest in the city, shaken by wind. The garden made a zoo for trees, where I had stood outside, circled the block, reaching up to touch twigs that dangled over the pavement. Inside waited a freedom of green. Then the morning aged, the Garden was opened, and I went through the whirling cage of the gate to wander. First I read the sign: "The Garden is a living museum. Please do not damage or remove plants." Then the map displayed the place: heaths, ash trees, azaleas, dogwoods, butterfly bushes, honeysuckles, willows, witch hazels, snowdrops, ferns, conifers, beeches, wisterias, iris, hollies, crab apples, hedge wheel, cherry walk, fragrance garden, children's garden, Shakespeare garden, local flora. I heard cicadas yammering in the elms, a hot siren wail, a jet plunging toward La Guardia, a sprinkler shaking water over the lawn, a cardinal calling its watery song from the cedars.

The brick wall brought me back to the alley in January. Snow came around the corner to swirl at my feet. A newspaper came billowing. Two men were starting down the street toward me. The wind instructed me not to pause.

Down by the river, at the vacant promenade, I stared west through falling snow at the glacial slab of Manhattan's city lights. Across the water, the trunks of the twin Trade Towers rose up. The bridge spun its webbing broad over time, to lift itself free from earth. Then the snow thickened and I stood numb with fatigue beneath a young sycamore. I wanted to dwell there long enough. The dark deepened. Long enough for full thought. All about me the architecture was old, but this sycamore was young. It lived in an artful well cut into pavement, where the trunk was surrounded with elaborate cast-iron grates that could be lifted away in sections as the trunk thickened. The bark, peeling forever in the custom of sycamore, was carved with many names. It was a museum of one being, a guardian of one circumference. I wanted it to outlive everyone.

What do I know of Long Island? Very little. At the heart of the mind, a healing memory may flourish. At the city's heart, a few trees hold sway. I can never keep myself from reaching to feel their furrowed bark with my fingers.

In my learning now, I abandon the middle distance. I am very close, on foot, touching the trees, or very far away, seeing two geographically distant islands at one glance. I see trees intensely by walking Brooklyn and thinking of wilderness; I see the city by entering the wilderness and calling Brooklyn back to mind. Three thousand miles west and four months later, I was on Long Island again.

Crossing to Long Island:
Willapa Bay

Now I want to take you to this other place called Long Island, a wilderness bump on the water off the coast of Washington state. There I was a guest of the old-growth forest for a night and a day. This island is set in Willapa Bay, and is seven miles tip to tip at high tide. It has no house, no bridge. The only access is by company ferry for the log trucks, or by canoe.

Two hours west from my city of Portland, I came to the landing on Highway 101 at midnight, slid the canoe off the roof rack, and staggered with it to the water. My job, my office packed with projects, had kept me until long after dark, and then released me with a shrug. Rolling the hull down into the ebb-tide mud, I straightened my bones and squinted at the dark of Long Island, three hundred yards across the channel. Even by day it's a dark shape, all cedar, hemlock, fir, yew. Now it was a dim hump below the stars.

A few quick strokes from land, I felt closer to the stars than to the road. I aimed north along the shore, where the narrow channel widened to miles of open water. A light breeze had come up. I pushed into it, trying to keep the prow's blade centered into the wind. Somewhere out on the flat of the bay the wind died, and I drifted, gazing about. Not a glimmer on the whole horizon, until a car came whispering down 101, its lights sweeping over the bay from the paved thread of the curve, then following a dwindling path back into darkness. From where I rested on the water, the whole horizon of my world was still.

My theory of destination collapsed. Where should I want to go, being already in place between the lull of water and the dome of stars? I peered over my shoulder toward where I had left the car on that highway. Then I gazed forward into the dark. What made my skull pivot to look back toward the car, toward that century, America, a life of longing that leads to this moment, when the wind and tide pluck my canoe into the actual world? I was glancing back at my car is if it were a coffin that had conveyed me to this point of change. I had sprung outward by starlight into another life.

I worked the paddle by feel, stroking the water's pelt, feeling the wind nudge my hull at times, and burrowing into the deep to bring the canoe around. Now fatigue was a pleasure, and time was gone, was a rhythm that healed me. The wilderness settled over me there, for wilderness is a place where the props of survival have dwindled to a few, and you know it. I lay down in the canoe, felt a little wavesplash wet my back, and for a time, let the wind lift waves against me, the long slot of the gun-

wale turning across the stars. At some point, I rose and paddled back to the center of something on the water, then turned toward the dark shape of Long Island and made for land.

A sunlit hummingbird buzzed to the spruce branch above me when I woke, with a wisp of lichen in its needle bill. I felt its lyric resiliency, its evanescent speed. Its tiny nest was a knob among the twigs there, and the bird worked to weave its small cup full. The bird was ruby and jade, with a glister of emerald. I watched the thumb-sized blur weave, and whizz away, and then spiral back with a buzz, work, and speed away. After its fourth departure, I stepped uphill toward the grove. The trees let down dim light, and a silence filled the forest room where I clambered up the slope through deadfall.

The old-growth cedar grove covers close to three hundred acres of high ground near the island's south end. Later, I learned an official refuge trail had been made at the grove's north end. Visitors today should stay on that trail. I swam in ignorance through the wet, tangled thicket of salal bush. It flourished seven feet high, and covered the slope. Its red stems buoyed me up, let me down with a crash. I flailed, parted the weave of it all by hand and tried to sidle through, dropped flat, feet in the air, stood, dove, rolled across half a mile of this salal that guards the grove along its south border. I was more seal, more fish. Some places the elk had pushed through. I followed their ways, until those dwindled and I was climbing twigs again, clutching at leaves, and tumbling. At one place, where a falling tree had torn open a square yard of mud, I found the print of bear, and of elk, and of raccoon. Each came there since the last rain—one day. And I swam on.

My stroll in the grove was more like a swim—dropping to a salamander crawl under shade-killed limbs, stepping onto mossy logs that gave way, slapping through salal to walk on, hip-high off the ground. As I paused to let steam rise from my salty face, I thought of the flower shop in lower Manhattan one day at dawn, where I met bunched salal, sword fern, and cedar from Oregon, the jade-solid greens bush-pickers had airlifted east for the weddings and funerals of the multitude.

Where the slope steepened, salal bush gave way to spindly young spruce, a darker impenetrability of shade-killed twigs and silence. In the spruce thicket I closed my eyes, and simply leaned and kept leaning through. I shaped my hands like prayer, and divided the bare twigs, burrowing a path through the sunless mass for my body. At one point I climbed the tallest spruce sapling I could grope my way to, and looked around from thirty feet up. Somewhere near, I could hear the growl and shouting of a logging show. The deafening business of the yarder would rev up, and die away, and then I would hear the working calls of the crew: "Where's the old man? . . . A little more gain!" And the yarding spool growled as it took up the slack on a cable. I felt fear in my belly against the trunk. I was on private land. There were surely signs somewhere barring me from entering, and if the company men caught me, I didn't know what would happen. Swaying where I clung to the spruce top, I felt like a squirrel in someone's sights, or a sitting duck.

Overhead a cloud was forming, gathering fog wisp out of the trees, billowing into being, turning, fattening, traveling east, settling against the tops of the cedar grove where it rose up from scrawny second growth, and pushing into the tall bare trunks of cedar and hemlock there, feathering through. The yarder revved again, buried in its work, something crashed, and I slid down into the dim realm of the thicket to flail, to fight and tramp the long way around where the loggers worked.

The next hour was a blur of toil, punctuated by moments of study: twig weave before my face, spider web across my face, snail unfurling beside my stalled foot, soft old stump with springboard notches. Finally, steaming with sweat, I ran up against a log thicker than I was tall, scrambled up onto it, walked its length, and came out in the open tangle of the cedar grove itself.

I was in it. The shadows of the grove closed over me like a thicket in the Brothers Grimm, but older than the Old World. Shadow was a robe of fragrances, threads of light a revelation I could taste. The intermittent shaggy stands of the oldest trees gave a pleasure of settled mass to every smaller thing, to salal bush palm-up everywhere, to sword fern splayed in whorls, to mushroom, to the rusty blur of the towhee winging through huckleberry thicket, to moss, lichen, gnat.

Under the tall crowns of hemlock and cedar, the old-growth grove of Long Island flourished with all sizes and soft geometries of green. These trees were dense, but yielding. The cedars and hemlocks themselves stood co-dominant, sharing the overstory. Hemlocks had fattened to five feet through at breast height, and they probably reached five hundred years in age. At a maximum of eleven feet thick and a thousand years, the cedars had assumed a candelabra shape, thick at the base, with a fast taper to a spindly top at around a hundred feet, where sparse and wind-shattered crowns raveled into a few large limbs branching into multiple spires. The forest was thick, but light broke through to trees at all stages of growth, from seedlings to ancient snags. I was in a congregation of children and grandmothers.

A cedar in this grove might live for a thousand years, and then stand as a snag hospitable to nesting woodpeckers, owls, and other birds and pioneer plant species for up to another hundred years, then fall and host many generations of plant growth on the ground. A downed log in this forest might linger five hundred years before it finally crumbles flat to soil. During this tenure, the tree would work as nurse log, a raised soggy bed supporting a throng of seedlings, and as a pool-forming barrier to streams, as a sunken boundary for shrews and voles, but a raised pathway for rambling mammals like me. Strict botanists have pointed out that the living layer of a tree's cambium, the one part of a trunk that lives—is only one cell thick. Only one percent of a tree is actually alive, they say. Yet the broader view calls all of the tree a living part of the forest long after that thin life layer withers and the tree stands dead, then falls. An individual tree may serve as a working part of its grove for a millennium alive, and half a millennium silvered by rain, dressed in moss.

I thought of my grandmother's character working in me twenty years after her death, her passing on. The euphemism is more accurate than the brutal word. She will not be all the way dead while I live, fed by her stories. In the family grove, we share everything.

Deep in the grove I suddenly had the feeling I was being watched. I turned, crouched to see through the tangle, scanned the green, and saw what had addressed me: ten feet up on a broad cedar trunk, a dark, square notch. My breath left me. This mouth, or eye, stared. Something older than my country was studying me. When I approached it, I could see this notch had been cut centuries ago, and the tree had curled new growth about it, trying to heal. I perched where I could to see inside: the strokes of an adz blade struck from the right, the notch tapering neatly the distance from elbow to fingertip toward the heart of the tree. I looked up along the trunk but could not tell if it lived. The overstory surrounded this trunk with so many colors of green, I couldn't tell which cloak the tree wore.

Maybe someone was looking for a sound canoe cedar. Maybe someone was making an eye to see me, to see what would become of the forest. I turned over my shoulder to look where this eye looked. I can't say how: the green world came into my face then. I had to climb down, stand apart. Somewhere over the grove, I heard the croak of two ravens. I saw them wheel above the crowns of the cedars. A south wind moved the highest branches. On the ground, I tasted the damp air, something smoky in the dense life of the place, as if growth were a burning that flamed green. I opened my mouth, but not for a word.

In the rich gloom I thought of the three cedar totem poles in the Brooklyn Museum, the Haida poles carved with a raven, an eagle, and a bear. Those poles had spent some time in the rain, somewhere, and their wood beaks and paws were nibbled by rot. Then, captured, they stood silent in their tall, dim room in the city. The living cedar of Long Island stands hard, even when stripped of bark. The oldest trees live until they are killed, by fire, catastrophic wind, the saw. Death is not in them; it comes to them.

I moved away from the tree with the notch, and lay down on the moss to close my eyes. The day began to blur. Time raveled out from a line to a constellation. I nibbled the sweet root of fern and inhaled crushed cedar. I was many sensations inhabiting one moment. I rose and rambled. The joints of my knees and hips, the snake of my spine, my neck frond turned limber as fern. I stood inside a hollow trunk, where light came golden through a tall crack, where drops of water came from somewhere far, far up in the dark to whap my tongue, to feed me the pitch and earth and pollen flavor of cedar. I rambled forward, or backward, through time. Was I thirty-nine, or was I wood? When I stood, I leaned. Everywhere, the oldest trees rose white as stone. Many stood bare, but hard—white cedar wood that rang when struck. I felt the urge to climb them, scaling up the chimney crack, gripping every available knuckle of wood and toe-hole niche to the top. Yet my boyish curiosity was rank impertinence, and I curbed it. I was a guest. I would ease through the thicket, step gently over moss. A mosquito landed on the sweat of my wrist. I poked my finger through moss to mud. By some whimsy of geology and weather, granite pebbles lay everywhere atop a meadow of moss. Outside a hollow trunk I found a heap of bones—the shoulder blades and ribs of a deer. Farther along, I touched an antler fragrant with mushrooms.

At the heart of the cedar grove I perched on a mossy hump to gaze upward along the white columns of the old ones, so perfect in gnarl and calm I wanted to be their child. My family tree could be cedar, branching from mineral soil, through duff, to seedling, to sapling, to me. When I was a child, my book about Daniel Boone ended with someone my size, small and amazed at the edge of the forest, with the loving, parental voice on the page saying, "Daniel, Daniel Boone . . . Someday you, too, may hear the forest calling your name." I felt a clutch of desperate patience then, sitting on the couch between brother and sister.

When! When would I hear it? That night under the old maple tree in the backyard, I began to listen. I heard some bird stir, or maybe it was the tree itself.

Since then, that voice has grown complex. I entered the grove, and it spoke with color and a pitchy fragrance, was built of a small bird's question and the wind's damp gift. The voice came now from the forest in an utterance braided of chlorophyll and fog, gritty with soil at the rooted blanket of moss and dank with a crumb nibbled from fern root. In the forest, I had many parents rising up above me. I wanted to learn their poise, their dignity, their readiness for change or a century without change. In the cedar grove, I held still. Its voice breathed my name—all our names—with an exhalation from the trees, where I perched on a mossy hump at the heart of the grove to gaze. On my bump of moss, I watched light flicker on a stream, water unraveling its cool skin from beneath a log, opening for a dozen feet of free run, then burrowing and gone under the roots of a massive standing cedar. Its surface worked flat in a mosaic of greens, a luminous glaze of dimple and swirl. Water was the eye that saw it all, saw the forest whole, one living shimmer. A spindle of sunlight broke through for a moment, penciled a thread on the water, and disappeared when a tree somewhere leaned back into place. The water carried a chill fragrance from the earth.

I stared deeper into the green thicket, trying by my life's compound eye to know another way of seeing.

The Nurse Log's Cloak and the Dwelling of Caddis

In the cedar grove, light shifted, and I dissolved backward, remembering a day on Knowles Creek, up the Siuslaw River from the Oregon coast. I stood ankle-deep in the water there to watch the caddis fly beginners fingering along over the rubbled streambed. They touched the stones where they walked hardly at all, buoyant and dancing along with a kind of tipsy assurance. Perhaps each held a bubble inside, to give its walk that jaunty ease. Many moved over the stones, their legs spidery with purpose.

I plucked one gently from the stream to study its self-made case: its coat, its house, burrow, cell? No word quite describes the sticky tube the caddis constructs about itself. With a twig I turned this one over in a bead of water on my thumb to list the makings of its cloak. First I recognized the stubby black of a hemlock needle, then the slate flakes of leaf, maybe year-old alder or maple, and a thread of moss, a tiny frond of something purple, dark pebbles of sand, a jewel of mica, some soggy filament which could be root, or a water-softened fiber of wood. It all fit together as the forest fit together. Knowles Creek tumbled about my feet, chilled numb, and I felt how my feet fit the round stones of that place better than any shoes.

As I squinted at the caddis in the gloom, my eyes resolved into focus beyond on a log by the stream. The loggers who worked the Knowles Creek drainage had left it somewhere upstream, the big butt swell of a hemlock or fir trunk, five feet through at the heavier upstream end, and twenty feet long. Still holding the recognizable shape of a log, it had softened inwardly to what we call a nurse log, a soggy bench better lit than soil, rot-softened and always wet. In deep forest, it is generally on the nurse log that a tree's seed, dormant through the winter, feels the sweet chemical tongue of water when spring warms it, and the tip of its embryo splits the seed case, turns down, chooses a place, and begins to lift a first green leaf.

I dipped my hand in the stream, the caddis walked away, careening past a mossy stone, and I splashed my numb feet across the stream to study the neighborhood of creatures harnessing the log, the small forest in a row.

The trunk lay thick, perhaps half a century dead where I put my hand on its damp flank. In its twenty-foot length, I counted what I could of that one log's population of greens and purples and reds: a clump of sword fern unfurling, wild iris blooming, fringe cup, thin-vined blackberry trailing down, the white bell blossoms of salal, the greenheart leaves of wild ginger popping up in a row, wild strawberry, five small hemlock trees with their bent heads swaying, a wand of cascara, one fir seedling knee-high, coast huckleberry with red fronds of furred new growth, Solomon's seal, tall and slender nettle, red huckleberry with its thin leaf circles of light, some small star-faced leaf I didn't know, inside-out flower, bunchberry, lacy grasses dusty with pollen, tiny cups rising from lichen, a whole small pantheon of mosses, and the thin leaves of rue. A solitary bee came humming down to enter a crevice, dressed in a blur of light. A long banana slug's calm progress left a shine. A cloud of gnats defined a favorable sphere of air. Two carpenter ants met, touched heads, went back the way they each had come, one up a fuzzy stem of thimbleberry, and the other into a neat round hole.

The caddis had walked the streambed, carrying its mosaic house, a miser of plain things. The log lay on the bank, a miser of creatures. The caddis held life inside, with a husk of debris. The log was dressed in a gown of life outside, with a core of inert punky wood. Each was a hull knit cleverly. The architecture of the forest begins with an accumulation of detail. The forest builds itself from the logic of this abundance, a teeming balance between the surge of growth and busy decay. In old-growth stands, a fallen log may seem more alive than a standing tree. This log by the stream shimmered. It lay like an ark carrying many lives forward past death into the next generation.

On the sun-warmed log, I lay on my belly among the mosses and felt the rush of its whole being, the entire pur-pose of the log and its citizens. The hum of sunlight spoke like a throb of music in the neighborhood on a hot night, when neither the children nor the grandmothers can contain their exuberance to be alive together. Insect buzz and blended flavors crowded about me. I touched my tongue to the moss and felt this rush in my own belly. I felt the green urge to make too many that is the urge that makes enough.

DOUGLAS FIR

WESTERN HEMLOCK

"SILVER THAW"

OLD GROWTH FOREST

OLD APPLE

COTTONWOODS

LOMBARDY POPLAR

WHITE OAKS

CHERRY

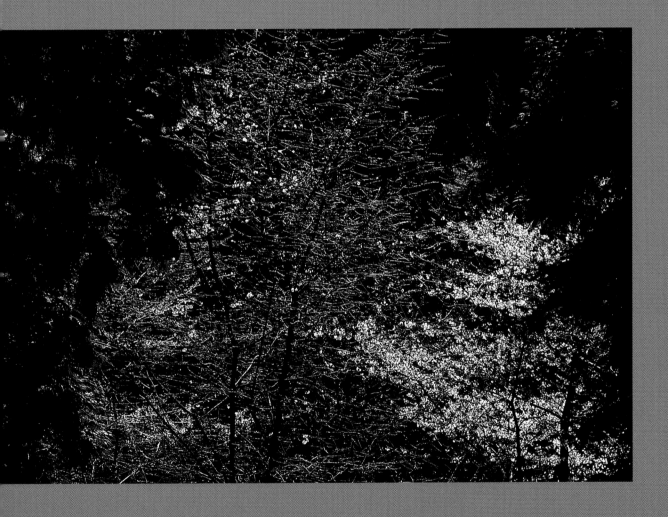

HEMLOCK AND SPRUCE

MOUNTAIN HEMLOCKS

SPOTTED OWL

COASTAL BRITISH COLUMBIA

ELMS

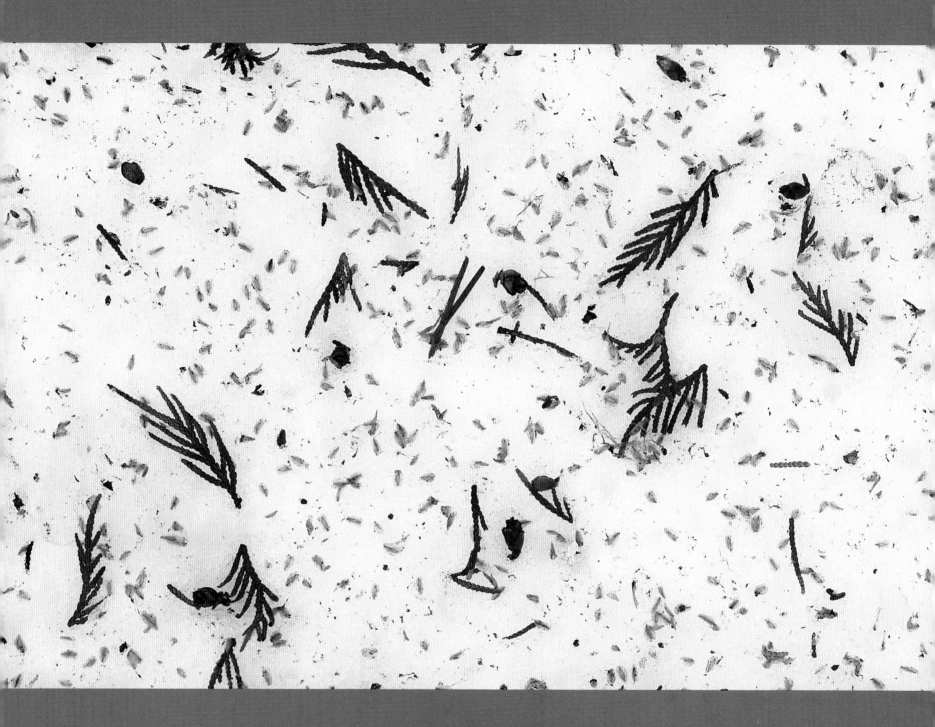

CEDAR SEEDS

Local Flora, Weather Permitting

In the cedar grove of Long Island, a young hemlock of about eighty years had toppled against one of the oldest cedar trees, and leaned where it lodged in the fork of the upper limbs. Both trees still grew. I scrambled, panting with vertigo, fifty feet up the oblique trunk of the hemlock. At every dangerous twist in the climb, I paused to dangle, to fit my body through bristling branches, to trust and not trust by the exact complexion of each limb's wood skin, until I arrived at the fork to study the upper world of the grove. There was a place where the limbs splayed out thick, where I could weave my legs and arms through branches and so lean back, knowing I would not unravel fast enough to fall, even if I slept. Salty sweat beaded my face. Sun dazzled my eyes.

Once there, I looked down, out, up, and closed my eyes. In the pack that hung from a limb stub by me, my Audubon guide to the *Western Forests* lay ready to explain what I saw. Somehow, I did not wish to open it. A book in the wilderness seemed an impertinence. On the ground, I had opened the book to learn more about that local exotic, the yellow banana slug, the six-inch hermit of slime and silence traveling smoothly over a log. When the book could tell me nothing about this humble creature, I had put the book away and taken the slug onto my hand. The unfurled eyes of the slug yearned forward on their slender stalks, as its long foot climbed across my palm, pausing now and then to nibble the salt of my skin with its tiny cat's-tongue rasp, to wrinkle its face closed and jerk down its eye-stalks, hold a deep thought, then unfurl again and glide on. As it moved its yin-yang swirl about my hand, the single nostril on its right side opened and shrank. Its glide made even the wrinkled travel of a snake seem boisterous. When I set it down on the log, it seemed to know my shadow, and shied from me, coasted over a crushed hackle of moss, then turned to slip away under a flitch of bark.

High on my perch in the hemlock, I tried to look about me without needing many names. Without the immediate boundary of the ground, I felt the full symphonic hug of air. I felt fear twist my belly every time I looked down, sixty feet of straight drop, and then the twin sensation of exhilaration when I looked around, turning my head as a bird might. A small bird sang, bobbing on a twig beside me. It hung upside down a moment, then tumbled and flickered to another twig. My hands felt like clubs. Red earth crowded a knothole in the living tree, welling from the rotted interior where limb-fall had torn bark away. I crumbled a pinch of this red earth in my palm, finding an ant wing, a tiny red seed case, filament roots, small bleached feathers of moss. Soil was the elixir of the grove, the alchemical transformation that yielded life from death. Living cedar bark ran a river up the south face of the big trunk to a few branches still high above me. In that bark, a pattern of holes was beaded with pitch. I tasted a bead, leaned back, closed my eyes.

Behind my closed eyes I let my mind skip back to my favorite corner of the Brooklyn Botanical Garden, three thousand miles east on the other Long Island. Every morning there they open the oak gate with its bronze spiral of spiderweb, leave the padlock hanging, and allow the curious into the Local Flora Section, weather permitting. That two acres is reserved for the original plants of the region, set close and allowed to naturalize in a series of thickets and wet meadows. The paths are not paved, and only a few of the trees wear their names on small engraved plaques, like professionals at a conference. When I entered there, my sun-dazzled eyes softened to the happy gloom. Trunks and vines crowded close, and the air was thick with a damp green flavor. An oak leaf's shadow swiveled on a trunk of pine. Out of the bog, a snail left a gleaming trail, crossing a rotting cherry log that sprouted green leaves. Ferns rose up, birches swayed and bowed, club mosses carpeted what fell. A rabbit nibbled thin grass in a mossy dapple of sunlight, its veined ears lit through. I wondered how it evaded the guard dogs that patrol the garden every night. A couple came along behind me, pushing a stroller with a sleeping child. I felt the human urge to point out the rab-

bit to them, but then averted my eyes and shared the rabbit's stillness as they passed. I held still and let them drift away. The rabbit's whiskers twitched, and it waggled its ears.

I reached out to taste a blond bead of pitch from the band of holes a sapsucker had left in a juniper trunk. Everywhere, small posted signs were explaining the place: "Danger—Poison Ivy . . . Kettle Pond: A water-filled depression resulting from the melting of a partially buried ice mass from a glacier . . . Pine barrens: a shallow sandy soil of high acidity and low fertility . . . Please stay on walks." I wanted to read, too, the signs writ gently in chlorophyll and pitch, the rabbit's stillness, the snail's path of light.

My favorite spot was the damp circle of sunlit earth where a young cedar (*Juniperus virginiana,* its name-tag said) had died, bog-killed, yet held its small domain. The place made me homesick for old forest, where a dead tree is suffered to remain, a perch for beetle and wren. Standing before this tree, as still as the rabbit, as poised as the trunk itself, I saw the green-suited spirit of the place, a woman gardener slowly pulling a bundle of cattail reeds through the pond. Her hair was gray, and her pace fit the local grove, her eyes downcast. I fell in love with what she summoned, the Indian of the place, the older being. She looked up. Our eyes met. Two bumblebees faced off in the air between us, swung about, then buzzed away.

When the garden closed, when I dashed below ground at the Eastern Parkway subway stop, plugged my token into the chrome slot, and spun through the turnstile, it seemed odd to see no trees. My eyes felt starved for green. I searched the porcelain walls and dusty tunnels of that realm for something alive in place. In the concrete tunnel, I could not understand how the glaciers and sandy soil of this island invited my hasty culture into being. With a roar, a stirring in the scattered crowd, the graffiti dazzle of the subway squealed steel on steel to a stop, the doors slid open, and I saw wood. Where the heels of the hurried scuffed through linoleum, at two spots by every door and in the long heel-groove under each bench, worn plywood showed the grain and knotted swirl of its growth. I sat down inside, fit my heels to wood, lurched forward with everyone.

In the cedar grove, where I perched in the limbs, the mysteries of Brooklyn faded. I opened my eyes and let the colors of the grove spread their healing mosaic through me. Where I perched to daydream, all time dwelt concentric in me. I was simply a young mammal in place, reviewing my range. This wasn't the first time I had inhabited daylight at a tree's own speed.

The Beeches of Lilliput, and the Old Growth of Belle

In the cedar grove, trees and snags and fallen logs surrounded me in a maze of leaf, bark, lichen. In it, no one lived alone. No one lived without a working kinship to many. Above me, where I clung to the tree I had climbed, the white stone trunk of the cedar was naked of its own growth clear to the few gnarled branches at a hundred feet, just below where wind or lightning broke it off. But even on that vertical column, many species grew. At the wood shoulder left by a shattered limb, a hemlock sapling reached out toward light. From a woodpecker hole, red huckleberry sprouted, fanning the green wand of its leaves. Long threads of blackberry vine hung from a knot, enlivening the light with whorls of green leaf and white blossom. From a crack, some fern splayed, too distant up the trunk for me to identify. Moss dusted a burl.

Retreating slowly from its own full life, the cedar hull and its passengers held together the forest's chlorophyllic rush. There was a principle to the green mosaic of the place, where leaves made shade, the wren made song, and my mind made stories. In that place, the forest began to teach me how the oldest things die, and yet live. When laughter ends, our definition of happiness must grow larger to include what follows. The withering of the last green twig or leaf signals another stage of generosity. Life is a frisky wisp that sometimes frolics in the mask of death.

From my perch in the cedar grove, I let my mind reel out its line. Just as this one grove harbored a diversity of lives, so my mind opened a fervent meadow of associations. My mind traveled in place, from the quirky riddles of the language itself, to a beech grove in Ireland, to the bristlecone pines of California, to the house-trailer parlor of Belle, the oldest woman I have known.

When I am among old trees, I am mute, but words rush through my mind. The cambium tissue of my brain, too, is very thin and incredibly busy. I remember my Nez Perce friend telling me about her people's names for trees. Of course, she said, they had names for the different species of their inland country, the poplars, cedars, firs, and pines. But they also had names for certain classes of heroic individual trees. One name meant a tree living off by itself guarding an isolate shade. This could be a timberline pine, or a gnarled poplar alone by the river. One name meant a tree old enough to hold moss on one face. One name meant a cedar mature enough to give its roots generously for the making of baskets. One name meant a tree that had given its inner bark for food when the people were starving. Such trees summoned stories, and were honored by them. A forked tree was known as twins, and must never be harmed.

Beside this respectful and detailed vocabulary, my culture seems limited at first. But I want to delve again to the roots. I grew up with the name "virgin timber" for any trees in the Oregon territory older than American history. Now the favored terms for that generation are "old- growth" and "ancient forest." Early loggers sometimes called a big tree "he." A trunk with high dead limbs likely to fall they called a "widow-maker." A tree that forked into two trunks they called "schoolmarm," and left standing when they hauled all the others to the mill. The name is erotic and misogynist at once. The name says more about the loggers than the trees, something lonely and funny and straight.

There is something true about calling this community of first trees both virgin timber and old-growth. An old-growth forest is very young in its busy ways, its fervency of growth. Yet at the same time it is old, fully accomplished in its ability to be young, to burst from its own death. It is precisely the fallen logs of an ancient forest that focus the grove's regeneration, so that grown trees may show the stiltlike base where they began by straddling a thick log now long gone.

Our word "original" once meant something that had existed from the origin of time. As recently as the eighteenth century, "an original idea" was a thought honored by time, burnished by the centuries. Since the Romantics' cult of the self and the torque of our own Revolution, "an original idea" has become the opposite of old—something utterly new, something no one has known before. We seem to love ideas not yet tested, as a child loves new toys. But old-growth forest is original in both senses. It was always there; it is just coming into being. Origin keeps happening. A square foot of forest duff, where the old leaves decay, holds more tiny creatures than the human population of Earth. And this density of life, this "biomass," extends to the shaggy communities of twig, lichen, insect, and rain where the old trees crown out hundreds of feet in the air. The array of life the nurse log suckles is but one visible episode of intensity in the whole busy weave of the grove.

Both virgin and nurse, the hospitality of an old tree is like the crushing embrace of a grandmother starved by absence from her young kin. But the embrace continues in the presence of those kin for centuries. Books and grandmothers teach me how to see the trees, how to leave my words behind and enter the grove. I read a tree's gesture, an old one's silence.

Once, on a bicycle, a little tipsy with Guinness beer, blighted by a tourist's fatigue and lost a day's ride west from Dublin, I came to the sign for Lilliput. I was following a narrow road already, and hadn't seen a sign in miles. By the sign's small, blue arrow, Lilliput lay off along a lightly traveled dirt track. Away through the dusk I went. Scrub brush rose into forest, my path dwindled, evening light dimmed, and I was among great beeches, their dark, wide trunks making my puny confusion fade. They kept a polite spaciousness from trunk to trunk, yet the canopy showed only thin seams of light. With these trees, I had a sense of great things dwarfed. The great island of Ireland itself seemed within their authority. And soon the stars would make small even the great trees themselves. I felt I rambled inside the hills, riding the path by twilight. I lay down on dry leaves, stretched below the sky web of limbs. Green light rushed down, and leaves twinkled in a light breeze.

As I lay in this trance, I heard a distant whine. An insect? Machine. I rose and followed it over the hill, and down a ravine where the sound grew louder, until I came to the little lumber mill, shack upon shack connecting together into a long assembly line that raveled down the canyon. No, it was a disassembly line, for I saw the giant logs of beech slide in at one end, and a stack of furniture billets rattle out the other. A man with a winch wrestled the great trunks onto a little railroad car at the uphill door, and at the mouth below, another man raked the spindles and rungs and chair legs into heaps. Both men tipped their hats to me. The whine of the mill was too loud for words.

I felt like a mosquito, a Lilliputian wrath. What could I do? I walked back over the hill to lie under the broad trees again. Soon, the stars would come out, but my bed in the leaves had grown cold. I was sober, and I was afraid.

I fear my own kind. I fear the impulse I tasted when, as a Boy Scout, I felt my ax bite wood, and a great alder came crashing down in a flurry of leaves and splinters. I try to remember that taste when I sit silent among the old ones now, among the beeches of Ireland, among the cedars of Long Island, among the bristlecones of California. On a great beech trunk, an old writhe of bark crawls like a wave arrested where it has gnawed a cliff. What makes time stand still like that? How does life last longer than the felt generations of human history?

Some say the oldest living creature may be a scrubby heather patch high up in Norway, whose seed lay frozen through the ice age in a lemming's burrow, then sprouted a paltry half millennium ago as the cold-fisted grip of permafrost thawed slowly northward. The sprouting of the shrub may have coincided with the Italian Renaissance, and its greatest flourishing with the Industrial Revolution. That seed became a bundle of stems, and each winter snow bent it back toward earth, until the plant quilted out over the entire hill, a flowered sprawl low on the ground. Small purple flowers have embroidered the hilltop every midsummer since the lemming's harvest. That shrub is ten thousand years old, by one reckoning. Or perhaps lichen is older, a fuzz on stone that never found reason to die, but crept one century to the inch across a horizon of granite. I hold moss between my fingers, and ponder the chaotic successions of lichen. But to learn about age, about how to stand with grace through time, I keep coming back to trees.

Once I went looking for old age among the bristlecone pines. Climbing to the White Mountain bristlecone grove on the California-Nevada line, my car ran out of air at ten thousand feet and coasted to a stall. Five A.M., October, and cold. I got out slowly, gulping air, gasping, stepping carefully as an old one. At the Patriarch Grove, white dolomite bruised my eyes like snow, and the trees twisted up from it, in small clusters and alone. A friend had told me this was the ugliest forest he had ever seen: scraggly trees, and not enough air for a decent walk. And I had the wrong book. My copy of *Forest Trees of the Pacific Slope*, compiled by the chief dendrologist of the U.S. Forest Service in 1908, concluded of the bristlecone, "On account of the poor form of the tree the wood is of no economic use; sometimes employed for minor local purposes in the region of greatest abundance. Longevity—Little is known of the ages attained. Trees from 16–20 inches in diameter are from 200 to 250 years old."

The chief dendrologist, for all his persistent field study, still had some things to learn from trees. But it was good to read his book there, to close the book and look upon the grove where the oldest known tree in the world still grew. The sprawl of wood they have named Methuselah is a single bristlecone pine that began its life around 2600 B.C. As I stared at this survivor, I thought of the Sequoia they named the Mark Twain Tree, with its ninety-foot circumference where two men chopped for thirteen days to make the undercut in 1891, felling the great trunk for an exhibition stump and fenceposts. I thought of the limber pine in Idaho, 1,550 years old, showing the slowest growth of any tree on record. For a time the radial growth on one branch averaged just over an inch per thousand years.

In the Patriarch Grove, nothing moved fast. I met a huge, soft rabbit that thumped about without concern for me. It did not run because it knew I could not. We shared a lunar etiquette: breath first, always breath, then an oblique glance at each other, then a turning away. I turned to the trees then, the twisted trees that had lived on the hill for four thousand years. They held fast to stone where the air was too thin for fire, the seasons too dry for rot, and the soil too poor for so much as a stem of grass in competition. Trees about me came writhing out from white stone scree, twisted by that shaping dance between erosive wind and persistent growth.

I had to lean against the trunk there, close my eyes, stop my ears, and exhale all I had. I could be wood. That was why I had come there alone. I had no sufficient happiness in my life, and my wood soul found comfort clenched there in the cold. I felt like a hollow tree the wind had eroded to bone. I touched my lips to the wood. Life came back to me sweet, with the first small sip of wind. I had undertaken a small rehearsal for old age.

The oldest person I have known was a woman named Belle, living alone at ninety-six in a house trailer far up the North Fork of Oregon's Siuslaw River. Her hairnet kept the flower of white that topped her snug, and her face pulled inward like a cloud in haste. She rocked, and then stopped still when words came, her tongue jogging along in an easy torrent, and then she rocked again in silence. If an old tree could speak, she might give it voice. The day I visited her last, she told me a story about finding the little habits that encourage long life. But first she had to tell me sorrow, to teach me bitter things.

"There's no future for a person my old—er, my age," she said. "You can't half see, you can't hear, you can't share. Person comes to visit, all they hear me say: 'What is it?' The folks got me a hearing aid, and while the sound is light enough—er, loud enough, it isn't distinctive, you know. So I don't use it. I'm just practically what they call a vegetable."

"It's okay," I said. I was young, and I knew life can be sweet. "It's okay."

"What do you know, son?" she cried, grabbing my wrist. "What do you know about being old?" Her eyes blazed. "I take some of the most miserable falls. Out chopping wood last fall, I slipped and hit hard and lay most of a day, looking at the sky!" She dropped my hand, and stared toward the window. "Folks won't let me chop my own wood now. I never had the Gypsy foot, but I did like to walk. That's all done now. Friend says when a person gets to be my age, they ought to round them up and shoot them. Hah!" She stunned the air still between us. "I think so!"

"Did you go hiking in the early days?" I said. The

scowl of anguish left her face, as a cloud's shadow departs from a mountain. Her eyes opened, and she leaned toward me.

"What is it?"

"DID YOU GO HIKING?"

"Did I go hiking? Why, I had to look after my sheep, you know. They got clear over in that Cataract country, over the hill and down the gulch, and all that land was timbered. It started in to snow. I turned to go home, I didn't know where I was. You know how the trees will bend down, and nothing was familiar.

"I had a little shepherd dog that always went with me. I said, Rex, go home. He started off. I said to myself, You're not going right, but I'll follow you anyway. Maybe we'll come to a little stream or something, and can follow that down.

"But he *was* going right. Took me right home."

She leaned back in her chair then. She rocked like a tree nudged by wind, her face turned up toward the soft light of the window, her mouth a line. The story was a gift to me about how I might live as a tree follows light: "You're not going right, but I'll follow you anyway." And the fallen log nourishes its destroyers, and the upright trunk builds color toward the sun.

Belle lived the equivalent of old-growth cedar. I left with her voice beating gentle forever in my mind. I felt more ready to age toward the kind of fierce self-possession she knew. I felt ready to forgive myself, the way my own story will turn and be lost. Many times, in trouble, I have softly said to this life, I'll follow.

Camping by White River

When I woke in the grove, opened my eyes fifty feet up the old cedar where I had slept, I caught my breath, lost for a moment, glancing down at the green tops of young trees. Vertigo passed, but left a wavering thrill. Then I remembered: I was on Long Island, up a tree, longing. The quiet explanations that sometimes arise in solitude would not be purely mine this time. Why had my brother died? Why had he driven to the mountains, put his head in a bag at the tailpipe? When that didn't work, he took up a gun. The old will die, but this man had children, young ones. This man was a year older than me. I looked around. Bret? The sun was low. A ruby-throated hummingbird swung down to buzz me, then looped up along a tunnel between limbs, came diving again with a scolding note, and spun away. I climbed down the shade-killed branches to the ground.

On the ground, I staggered. My legs had stiffened, and I could have used some level ground. There was none. Scrambling through the grove at dusk, I came upon two saplings that had grown side by side, then splayed flat when a heavy limb fell on them. Their roots had torn from the earth with the blow, and they lay oblique, foot to foot where moss had begun to climb over them. I thought of my brother. I thought of Odin and his brothers Vili and Ve, walking along the bleak seashore shortly after the world began. The three found two fallen saplings, ash and elm, their roots ripped from the ground. Odin plucked them up, breathed upon them, and his brothers gave gifts that made these two the first man, Ask, and the first woman, Embla. From them, the old story says, descended all people—even Lif and Lifthrasir, who would hide in the Guardian Tree to survive the ice and fire of the world's end.

As I stared down at the two saplings, knelt between them, I felt I knew Odin's mind. But I could not understand my brother's. These two trees lay down to rest. I stood up. Beside me, a tree stood as my brother might, a trunk with limbs that reached out, beckoning, a relative who has turned away, hiding the face for a moment.

In the green tangle of the grove, I could find only one dark, plain place to stand, and that was inside a wide cedar trunk alive, but hollowed by fire. I had to go to my knees to wriggle inside, but then I was upright, tasting the damp air, looking up the hollow bore of the trunk to one white oval of light where flame had burrowed out to the sky. This tree, like every tree, protected the place of its origin, covered the dense, local darkness where its root first split around a stone. Maybe my brother's beginning still lived in me. I closed my fist. From seed so small a

salamander's moist hand covered it, this tree's mass rose to a distant glimmer of green.

Once, camping at White River with my brother in the rain, I dreamed I stood at the entrance to a great urban museum—all marble columns at the entrance, and great flights of steps leading to guarded doors. I asked one guard bristling with badges and a gun what might be inside. He knew nothing to tell me, he said. He shrugged, looked me up and down. He was suspicious of me, but still he let me through the bronze door, and I followed the corridor toward a lit room, an echoing space with the soft rustle of moving water and a damp wind. At the heart of the building was a forest, a dense green grove rising from the marble sill enclosing it, a stream freshening the air, a lush breathing of trees and fog. There came a rattle of songs from hidden birds. The tall skylight webbed with steel let down the white sun. There was a dream sense that no one understood this creature of green and bark and odor, but everyone knew it must be kept alive.

In that light, in that green room, I sat by the stream a long time. That place had the happy gloom of kindred trees, and water sliding by a stone. When I left, they asked me to put on new clothes. I would not need the old ones, they said. They would throw the old ones away.

Waking, I heard rain the trees shook down onto our tent. I heard my brother's slow breath. My brother, sleeping, had to be the spirit of the place—my mountain relative. Outside the tent, White River went rollicking over stones. I heard wind combing the long forest slope where we hid. In my bag in our tent under the pines, I wondered how to survive. The guard in the dream did not know about the forest inside, but did know the importance of securing the door. Once inside, I knew the trees were guarding him, keeping things whole. If part of the good luck of growing older is seeing the drama whole, then trees are the longest teachers of our time. There is a cairn for my brother in the mountains. Under a pine, I guard something of him I may never understand. At the end of a trail, he disappeared into the sun.

Back in the grove at Long Island I hunched in shade to dwell on a snail shell soft as ash, a green twig of cedar, a fallen spiral of bark, a moss fist. I took out the notebook that fit my palm to write some scrap of this. Sawdust billows out from the kerf when loggers and sawyers take a tree apart, when the headrig tailors a bundle of boards from heartwood. I would go the other way. I would fit small scraps of sensation into something whole, traveling at ground level through the thicket with tongue and ear and fingertip. I carry my city mind into the grove and feed it pitch. I sit by water. I inhabit a hollow tree. I try to be my brother, too, now that I have become the oldest. I sleep like a coon, saunter, stumble. I swim through the limbs leaving a trail of steam. When my mind is full, when my hands are thick with pitch, it is my time to leave the island. My brother is gone, but my love awaits me. She took her mother's ashes to a cairn of

her own in the mountains. From this, we have an understanding. My brother is gone, but a life awaits me.

At my landing where the hummingbird made a basket, I would make a basket, a knit swirl of cedar bark to hold some berries of salal. A basket, like a story, is the place where things cohere. It may seem crude, finding its own shape as it is woven, yet be sufficient to hold a fragrance, to fashion a pleasure, a twist of sorrow, a healing. Was I a proper inhabitant of the grove, moving out of my culture into something older, a night woven of tide, sleep, cedar? I would learn of cedar, woven into being by light. Finally, my learning was a small feast with a plain flavor.

I gathered my night of knowing, my season of belief. I plunged through the forest to the canoe in deep grass, untied the knotted bow rope from a spruce, dragged it to the water, set out against the wind. My paddle flashed in spray.

The Tree of Nine

When the archeologists pried open the door to Cheops' tomb at Giza, their first sensation was the odor of cedar that had filled the room for 4,600 years. A boat lay disassembled before them, just as the servants of pharaoh had laid it out for the funerary journey of their lord. The body of Cheops had been elaborately prepared for eternity, wrapped in cloth and spices. But the wood of the cedar boat was breathing still, incense its essence. Deep under the Great Pyramid that rises to greet the sun, cedar wood inhabited that stone room, prepared to be fit whole again and glide the Nile, or some great stream by which the Nile crawls like a thread below starlight.

That tomb was hermetically sealed by the best ingenuity of the kingdom, and no thieves found it. The treasures of the centuries were safe. And the Long Island grove? I think again of the great cedar trunk I had found with that square notch cut by the natives of the place. It proved sound for a canoe hull, but they never cut it down, never hollowed it with fire, nephrite adz, and elk-bone chisel. That hull still stands whole. The tree remains; the people have gone away.

On Long Island, silvaculturists estimate there has been no catastrophic fire for the past 4,000 years, no fire since the coastal climate dampened and the pines moved east. A few trees show the isolated mark of lightning strikes, but rain must have quenched them. Wind has spared the place. Hurricane and tornado have worked other landscapes on the continent, but the Long Island grove stands almost undisturbed. The cedars and their younger kin have been spared: hemlock, fir, salal, yew. It is doubtful we will ever again manage to leave a place alone this long. We will never make such a forest. Since my walk there, the grove has become a protected place, a Research Natural Area within the Willapa National Wildlife Refuge. Visitors are asked to stay on the trail that touches the north tip of the grove, and to leave the interior alone. The place has become a museum in the open, a three-hundred-acre tract boxed by timber cuts that flank its dense green heart. It is a place for study by professionals, a botanical library. Parts of it may be the small true wilderness where no one goes.

I have spent two nights on Long Island, east and west, and what do I know? I touched one small point at each place—Brooklyn, and a corner of the cedar grove. I would grow old, delving many times like this into the groves and glens of being. I travel to know the trees who do not move. How can I learn, with my culture, how to live?

They say there was a man who would ride his rattletrap bike through Central Park, stopping to fill his basket with horse manure, and then he would disappear down Fifth Avenue toward the lower east side. He wore purple and an odor, they say, and he followed the horse carriages that carried tourists under the trees in spring. If they ever looked back, they saw him with his scoop. Somewhere, in a dingy lot many blocks to the south, he was building Eden in a vacant lot of rubble and dust. He was building shade and birdsong, raising the blossoming trunks of small trees, watering apple saplings and mountain ash, coaxing morning glory up a sooty brick wall. They called him Adam. They called him foolish. I call him guardian of his own chosen place.

Eighty miles up the Hudson, on a bluff above the river stands the tree they call the Tree of Nine. Over a century ago, someone planted nine silver maple saplings in a tight ring on the lawn outside Blithewood Manor, and they are now grown by their busy cambium weld into one tree. On a summer day, together the Tree of Nine casts a welcome circle of shade, far out on the lawn alone. The young stroll out to it, but shy away from the poison ivy climbing its thick trunk, thistle bristling in bloom, sumac and willow sprouting at its roots, the carpenter ants trailing up the furrows of their prize.

Two strands of the trunk have died, but they are held upright by the others, wedded into one being. In mass, the Tree of Nine approximates one cedar trunk in the grove at Willapa Bay. It stands as a single curiosity, and has a name. This one tree, being old, being complex, invites me into its own local wilderness. The wild is right there—wild chances and processes where my finger touches thistledown grounded at a niche in the bark, due for sprouting. That's wilderness, a local complexity healing a place without us. The moment it ceases to be there, we are gone, for we are part of it.

I have spent important hours with the Tree of Nine, settled into the accommodating wood knobs and rooted bark folds at its base to watch rain veil the manor, the lawn, and the forest beyond. All about me lie the spent souvenirs of my people—a tineless plastic fork, a candy wrapper all of gold, half a shattered champagne glass, the punctured mylar holder for a name-tag, emerald green beer bottle, cigarette butt. I sit there now, writing this paragraph on a clipboard, shielding these words from the light rain with my bent head. A daddy longlegs crosses the page, pausing where the pen moves, sizing up my finger for danger or prey. In the furrows of the trunk at my back, and in the niches between roots twisting into the ground, I count inventory of the tree's guests—poison nightshade, poison ivy, sweet oxalis, licorice-root fern, embroidery moss, crabgrass, Virginia creeper, pigweed, dock. I hunch among the multitude of this place.

From the shade here, I gaze over the lawn at Blithewood Manor, once a genteel estate, then a college dormitory, and now in the throes of change. It is being gutted so a dwelling may be made, a proper residence and working retreat for a think tank of economists. I hope they will stand by this tree, in their deliberations, as they seek their vision for this earth, its true green being. Sometimes it takes genius to leave things alone.

One night near the Tree of Nine, the night before my frosted stroll over the Brooklyn Bridge to a few acres of Long Island, in the dorm at Bard College I woke and thought of that tree. It was ten below, and blowing hard against the window. The room had a chilled light from snow outside. I felt more sorrow in that place than I had ever known. I was a teacher there, or I tried to be. I remember one of my students announcing on the first day of class, "My name is Michael V. Bennedetto, III, and my parents have promised on the day I finish at this college I can have any car I want, and, frankly, I wish that day could be today." A ragged breath fled from me.

Why couldn't I laugh? Why didn't I invite the young man to stand and make his departure right then? That was August. This was January. I drank too much wine in Rhinebeck, and retreated to my room. I stood at the window a long time while the dorm grew still. Snow came whispering down outside. There was no point sleeping; life passes soon enough.

Bundled in everything I had, I walked the midnight road, finding a strange pleasure in the gusts of terror and cold that leapt from pine shadows, holding my hand against my face at the wind's bite, high-stepping the long drive built for carriages. And there it was, the Tree of Nine on the broad crust of the lawn.

It stood shorter in the snow, buried knee-deep, its broad, bare crown snapping in the wind. Something very old in me has loved old things, has made me loyal to places under siege. I clambered through the snow to stand beside it, then to grapple and hang, my numb fingers gripping the ice skin of the lowest branch. I fell into the drift, and then staggered upright, shook like a dog, reached, and finally swung up into the limbs.

Its life century had filled the core of The Nine with leaves, and I settled into the hollow of it, covering my nose with my paws to sip air, foxlike, snug. The cold had a thing to do, and I had a thing to do. The tree was the place.

There may come a time when our forests are reduced to a few hidden groves, like those Dawn Redwoods from the fossil record that appeared in a ravine in China, living as they always had, shaggy with thin leaves, swaying gently in the old work of the green world. We will know they are sacred, and hold the greatest living secrets of time.

Or this may be the decade when we waken. This may be the time we acknowledge the citizenship of trees. Looking back at us, our youngest grandchildren may say: "Those were the ones who entered the grove, and were changed."

A friend told me, "We are a people growing onward from this fascination with ourselves. We are falling in love with the earth." We take this choice not out of fear—though we might, for we die if the trees die. But we make this choice from the kindred sensation we share for Earth with trees. We feel we are gathered into the grove.

For every tree is the Tree of All Trees, not just in my vision, but the world. Every first leaf, every sapling rises up to claim the earth: This is my home. This is my rightful place.

They say that on that one day Chief Joseph was allowed to visit his native Wallowa Valley, before being returned to the desolation of the reservation, he cried out, "I ask only for a place to throw my blanket on the earth. Allow me this."

My people denied him. We said the syllable, No. He raised his head, and was led away.

Every creature asks only this: a place to throw a shadow on the earth, to root, to sip rain. This is not much, but everything. And now, we are the ones who say no, or yes.

If you stand in the fragrant shade of an old one, or by the thin shadow of a sapling, if the cedar waxwings fill the flickering birch above you, if Orion glimmers through an old elm after midnight, and you hold still long enough, you will be changed by magic into yourself. You will turn to another and see inside, kindred spirit in grief and laughter, heartwood open. Say yes to the Earth. You will enter the grove before dawn.

MAPLE LEAVES

COAST MOUNTAINS, BRITISH COLUMBIA

WALLOWA MOUNTAINS, OREGON

BIRCH

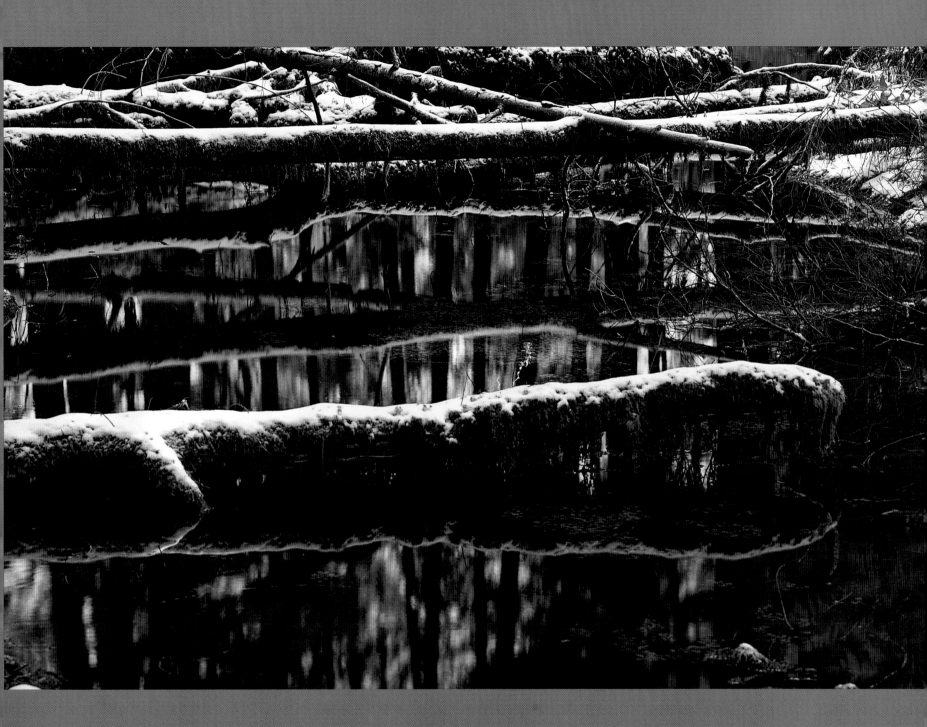

FOREST POND

EUCALYPTUS

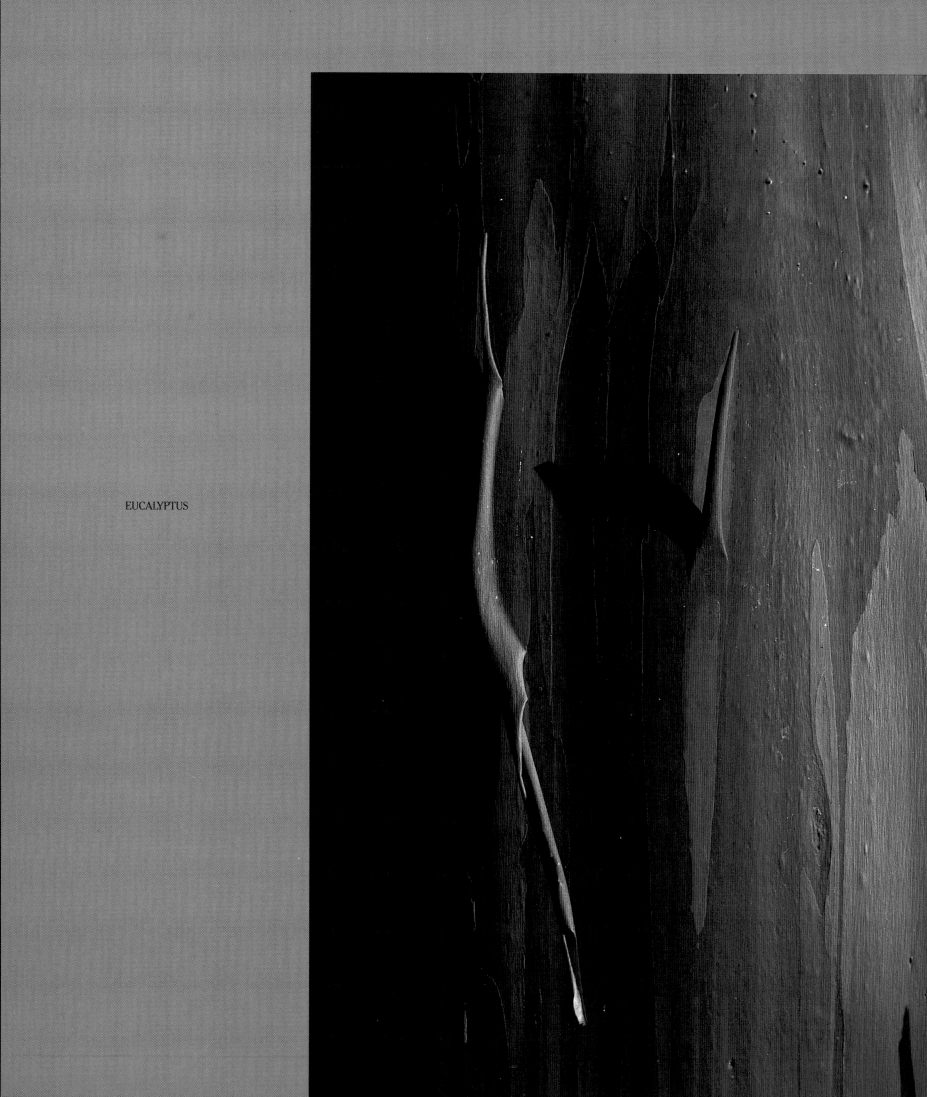

AMERICAN CHESTNUT STUMP

RAINFOREST COSTA RICA

BIG LEAF MAPLE

OAK AND BEECH FOREST

BIG LEAF MAPLE AND MINERS LETTUCE

WESTERN HEMLOCK SEEDLING

GREAT SMOKY MOUNTAINS

ALASKA TUNDRA

LIVE OAK

BEECH

PLANT A THOUSAND TREES

Or save just one. The earth needs more trees.

Individual trees are beautiful and full of magic through the seasons. As forests, they create landscapes of great complexity and antiquity that nurture more plants and animals than other ecosystems. Trees hold and shade the soil, reducing erosion. They take up carbon dioxide—each mature tree about thirteen pounds of CO_2 per year. They provide food and shelter for many creatures, including humans. But the Earth's forested land is already a third smaller than before the advent of human agriculture and industry, and is shrinking by about thirty million acres per year.

Rainforests, home for more than half the planet's terrestrial wildlife, are being destroyed by slash and burn agriculture, ranching, and logging at a pace estimated at fifty acres per minute—that's one square mile every thirteen minutes. Loss of trees and forests, especially our oldest, is also rampant in the United States and Canada due to logging beyond the sustained growth of our forests, urban sprawl, and acid rain.

Worldwide, much of the wood is burned, and we often don't use well the products made from trees. Each year Americans alone discard one hundred billion pounds of wastepaper. Half the paper consumed in the U.S. is used solely to wrap and decorate the products we buy— and most of that is discarded, to become one-third of the volume in landfills. Over a billion trees are used just to make disposable diapers each year.

New trees are being planted, but not nearly enough to make up for the losses. Each of us who cares about trees and forests must help reduce the waste and increase the number of trees through simple actions.

What You Can Do

Be conservative in your use of paper and recycle everything possible. Try not to buy items wrapped in multiple boxes just for show. Take your own shopping bags so you won't need paper or plastic at checkout. Eliminate or reduce use of paper diapers. At home and office, use both sides of paper and establish separate trash cans for clean paper, newsprint, and cardboard. Investigate and use recycling programs in your community. Ask unwanted junk mail advertisers to remove your name from their list.

Buy recycled paper for as many purposes as possible. Compared to "virgin" paper, making 100-percent recycled paper requires much less energy, creates much less air and water pollution—and uses no trees! Recycled computer paper, letterhead bond, wrapping paper, notecards and stationery, notebook paper, envelopes, copy machine paper, paper towels—even toilet paper—are increasingly available. Wherever you shop, ask for 100-percent recycled, unbleached paper, since the bleaching process can discharge pollutants—and keep asking until stores carry full product lines. Ask local businesses and newspapers if they are using recycled paper, too.

Be aware of where the wood and paper you use comes from, and avoid tropical wood and plywood, and imported paper. The United States consumes more tropical hardwood than any other nation except Japan, adding to the deforestation of rainforests. Your lumberyard, builder, furniture store, and paper dealer should be able to tell you the source of their wood products. Be conservative in all your uses of wood.

Plant trees in your yard, neighborhood, and city. Tree planting is healthy, enriching, and can be experienced by everyone. Trees in urban areas reduce air pollution and lessen noise and, if planted to shade buildings, can greatly reduce heating and air conditioning bills. Free and inexpensive seedlings are often available through state forestry programs, the National Arborday Foundation, and local environmental groups. After planting, make sure your trees have enough water, support, and care.

Become an advocate of trees and be aware of existing trees in parks and forests that may be threatened. Many older trees are in danger from acid rain, urbanization, short-sighted land use planning and overlogging. Join a conservation group that is working in your area and support it with money and/or time. Make sure it has a committee working to locate and protect stands of native, old, and endangered trees. Some national groups that have tree and forest programs are listed below.

The act of planting or saving a tree will give confidence that you can have a positive effect on the way of life of your family, the appearance of your town, and the future of the Earth.

Where To Get Information On Trees

Send along with your request for information a minimum donation of $10 to support a group—if you can. Then send more as you are able.

NATIONAL ARBORDAY FOUNDATION has as its only goal increased tree planting and tree care throughout North America. Programs like Tree City U.S.A. and Conservation Trees encourage individuals, neighborhoods, and towns to plant. Every $10 member receives free trees, and Arborday offers mail-order trees, too.

100 Arbor Avenue • Nebraska City, NE • 68410

AMERICAN FORESTRY ASSOCIATION encourages the planting of 100 million trees in cities and towns through its "Global ReLeaf" program. Maintains the official register and information on the largest individual tree of every American species.

1516 P St., N.W. • Washington, DC • 20005

RAINFOREST ACTION NETWORK links tropical forest preservation groups around the world. Produces newsletters, conferences, public events, and action alerts to protect rainforest everywhere. Especially active in promoting corporate and governmental responsibility for forests.

301 Broadway • San Francisco, CA • 94133

THE NATURE CONSERVANCY works with local citizens, corporations, and governments throughout the U.S. and Latin America to purchase and protect endangered landscapes. The Oregon office, for example, is purchasing private old-growth forestland adjoining Opal Creek, the largest unlogged yet unprotected valley in the national forests of Oregon. The Conservancy's International Program is buying tropical rainforest in Belize; a $30 donation buys one acre of forest.

1815 North Lynn St. • Arlington, VA • 22209

Oregon program • 1205 NW 25th St. • Portland, OR • 97210

CONSERVATION INTERNATIONAL also works directly with local groups throughout the tropics to encourage research and preservation of biological diversity in crucial natural ecosystems. Recently began programs in Washington State's Willapa Bay and the largest remaining temperate rainforests and estuaries of British Columbia and Alaska.

1015 18th St., NW • Washington, DC • 20036

EARTHSTEWARDS NETWORK practices citizen diplomacy through cultural exchanges among the United States, Soviet Union, India, Central America and elsewhere—notably by sponsoring international tree plantings by youths. Its Peace Trees project has planted thousands of trees in India, Costa Rica, and Nicaragua and encourages others to plant Urban Peace Trees in reclaimed city soil.

P.O. Box 10697 • Bainbridge Island, WA • 98110

TREES FOR LIFE, a part of the Findhorn Foundation, is in contact with hundreds of tree and forest protective organizations around the globe. Publishes Trees for Life calendars and encourages the planting, care and preservation of trees and all plants.

The Park • Forres IV36 OTZ, • Scotland

NATIONAL WILDLIFE FEDERATION, one of the largest conservation organizations in the world, is committed to the protection of the global environment. Places great emphasis on preservation of ancient forests and the conservation and reforestation of all woodlands as animal habitat.

1400 Sixteenth St., N.W. • Washington, DC • 20036

FRIENDS of TREES, TREEPEOPLE, TREES ATLANTA, and other local groups have a national reach in their attractive programs for reforesting the urban environment. TreePeople planted a million trees in Los Angeles before the 1984 Olympics and now has programs for tree maintenance, as well. Friends of Trees in Portland has gained the support of children, adults, local governments, and park administrations.

Friends of Trees • P.O. Box 40851 • Portland, OR • 97240

TreePeople • 12601 Mulholland Drive • Beverly Hills, CA • 90210

Trees Atlanta • 96 Poplar St., N.W. • Atlanta, GA • 30303

WORLD WILDLIFE FUND, dedicated to saving endangered animals and their habitats around the world, supports many tree-planting and forest-protection projects. Your donation can buy seedlings for villagers in Cameroon, defend the forested sanctuary of monarch butterflies in Mexico, and help residents of Nepal reforest steep Himalayan valleys.

1250 24th St., N.W. • Washington, DC • 20037

THE BASIC FOUNDATION coordinates with several Central American conservation groups like ARBOFILIA in Costa Rica and PRO NATURA in Mexico's Yucatan region to reforest tropical areas. Arbofilia, for example, trains subsistence farmers in nursery skills while the farmers plant hardwoods and fruit trees on deforested riverbanks, farms, and roadsides. A $5 donation plants one tree; $250 plants a hectare—about 1,000 trees.

P.O. Box 47012 • St. Petersburg, FL • 33743

TREES FOR THE FUTURE maintains a very ambitious and widespread program of global reforestation. Operates 2,000 village projects which plant more than 10 million trees each year. A $30 donation can provide enough seeds for a village.

P.O. Box 1786 • Silver Spring, MD • 20915

All national conservation groups, such as NATIONAL AUDUBON SOCIETY, SIERRA CLUB, THE WILDERNESS SOCIETY, and FRIENDS OF THE EARTH are working to protect forests. In tropical forest protection, RAINFOREST ALLIANCE and EARTH ISLAND INSTITUTE are also leaders. For more information on recycling, contact ENVIRONMENTAL DEFENSE FUND • 257 Park Avenue South • New York, NY • 10010.

Finally, there are several companies providing mail order sources for recycled paper products and other ecologically sound products. They also distribute information about recycling, energy reduction techniques, and conservation:

EARTHCARE PAPER CO. • P.O. Box 3335 • Madison, WI • 53704

CONSERVATREE PAPER CO. • 10 Lombard St. • San Francisco, CA • 94111

SEVENTH GENERATION • 10 Farrell St. • Burlington, VT • 05403

AUTHOR'S NOTE

The text of this book draws on stories and poems by many writers under the spell of trees, and I would like to acknowledge some of them here. Pablo Neruda's poem referred to in the first section is "Juegas Todas los Dias" and can be found in *Collected Poems of Pablo Neruda,* edited and translated by W. S. Merwin (Vintage, 1974). Readers can find the story of Odin and his brothers by the shore, a discussion of the Norse text of the *Voluspa,* and an account of the world tree, Yggdrasil, in Kevin Crossley-Holland's *Norse Myths* (Pantheon, 1988). A modern translation of the Old English poem "The Dream of the Rood" can be found in Burton Raffel's *Poems from the Old English* (University of Nebraska Press, 1964); my reading of the original text is from *The Dream of the Rood,* edited by Bruce Dickins and Alan Ross (Methuen, 1963). The etymological treatment of the words *tree* and *true* is drawn from the *Oxford English Dictionary.* The oral history interviews with Forrest Francisco and Belle Dick are from the collection of the Siuslaw Pioneer Museum in Florence, Oregon, where I did fieldwork in 1975–76. I am grateful to my friends in that community for their hospitality during my oral history work.

Two writers in particular have helped my understanding of old-growth ecology: Jerry Franklin and Chris Maser. See, for example, *Natural Vegetation of Oregon and Washington,* by Jerry F. Franklin and C. T. Dyrness (Oregon State University Press, n.d.) and *The Seen and Unseen World of the Fallen Tree,* by Chris Maser (U.S. Forest Service, 1984). The story of the opening of Cheops' tomb was reported in *National Geographic* in 1954. The story of Chief Joseph's visit to his home in Wallowa was told to me by the Nez Perce poet Phil George.

I am grateful to the caretakers of the Brooklyn Botanical Garden in New York and of the Willapa National Wildlife Refuge in Washington for their careful work in preservation and interpretation. Readers wishing to visit the path to the Cedar Grove should contact the Refuge Manager, Willapa National Wildlife Refuge, Ilwaco, Washington 98624.

I am grateful to many friends who helped me live the questions that brought this book into being. I am grateful in particular to Richard Cohn of Beyond Words Publishing, who first asked me to write 15,000 words about trees in two weeks, and to Gary Braasch, who has contributed ideas and challenges that have pushed me farther. I am grateful to my editor, Buckley Jeppson, and to Gibbs Smith for bringing the book to its present form. Beyond all others, this book is a tribute to my brother, Bret William Stafford (1948–1988), who led me into the forest and is my companion there.

Kim R. Stafford

PHOTOGRAPHER'S NOTE

I hope people will discover in these images their companionship with trees and realize how much they and the earth depend on them. Trees and shrubs, for most people in the world, are an everyday encounter, often central features in the landscape. Yet learning about my local woods and studying tropical forests, being witness to the daily destruction of trees wherever there is "progress," has convinced me that trees are undervalued in our society. Especially, we put insufficient value on wild trees—those out of the relentless control of orchards, street plantings, tree farms, and well-trimmed parks.

Trees are complex, sensitive, and long-lived organisms that cannot flee danger or seek new homes but survive in place, simultaneously in touch with earth and sky, accumulating as a result a deeply rooted intelligence. This is an intelligence borne of being the oldest and largest of all Earth's inhabitants. An intelligence that made trees so central to religion and myth. An intelligence that informs the growth, fruiting, and survival of every tree, including the ones we keep in yards, orchards, and plantations. We lose touch with the ancient, wild messages of trees only at our peril.

Photographing a tree is not as inherently difficult, perhaps, as photographing a wild animal or a grand landscape: it can't flee, nor does it span wide spaces. Yet trees are wild creatures. They have personalities and moods and are tenaciously inseparable from their surroundings. To get these attributes on film, one must often stalk or wait, as if to photograph an animal, and be attuned to the cycles of seasons, growth, and light as in landscape photography. Careful observation of trees reveals private landscapes and unimagined complexities which may require unusual effort, patience, or equipment to record on film. Here, then, is information about some of the trees and photographs in this book.

1. Tropical forest of La Amistad International Peace Park, a few miles from the Panamanian border, Costa Rica. This protected area was established by both countries, in recognition that ecosystems do not respect political boundaries but are profoundly affected by them. Photographed in a downpour, into afternoon light, with a 300mm lens.

2. View down into an old-growth forest of the Cascade Range as fog slips gently over a ridge, revealing the individual branching of the conifers, some of which may be over five hundred years old. The needles of these trees are adapted to combing up to thirty inches of water per year from fog. See also page 5.

4. An exposure of several seconds through a 105mm lens reveals the motion of both wind and water on the Swift River, White Mountain National Forest, New Hampshire.

10. In a swampy forest that may have been undisturbed by catastrophic fire or storm for four thousand years, a western hemlock seedling roots in the bark of an ancient cedar, Willapa Bay National Wildlife Refuge, Washington.

11. The blush of early spring accentuates the shape of each alder tree in this thick stand seen from above. Alders are important guardians of the soil following logging or fire in western North America, quickly reseeding and returning nitrogen to the soil.

13. A single large tropical-forest tree remains in this dawn view over the Sarapique region of the Caribbean slope of Costa Rica, much of which has been converted to cattle ranches and plantations. Photograph made with a 200mm lens.

15. Tenacious pines and junipers clinging to clefts and shelves in the wall of Yellowstone Canyon in a telephoto view from the west rim. There are few landscapes in North America totally bereft of trees, but sometimes one must search carefully to see them, just as the trees, seed by seed, have searched for places to root and survive.

36. When Jackson Pollock was asked if he painted nature, he reportedly replied, "I *am* nature." The energy that seethes in his works, especially the underlying colors like yellow, silver, and red that he nearly covered over as the paintings progressed, can be felt in the wild confusion of overlapping growth of a forest or thicket. Here it is alder branches contrasting with their shadows on the forest floor; on page 38, distant sunlit fall colors push between shadowed alder trunks; and on page 45 the energized backdrop is lichen-covered columnar basalt cliffs along the lower Columbia River in Washington.

46. The dogwoods of the Appalachian Mountains are threatened by a blight, apparently similar to the fungus that attacked the American chestnut earlier this century (see page 103). Losing the dogwood would mute the early spring in the tulip, oak, and maple forests like this one along Ramsay Prong, Great Smoky Mountains National Park.

48. Spring ephemeral wildflowers paint the Mojave Desert in a view through a 105mm lens. The Joshua trees are not true trees, of course, but are yuccas up to thirty-five feet in height inhabiting the niche that trees fill in other ecosystems.

68. "Silver thaw" is a local name for an ice storm which results when a warm front showers rain onto a landscape that has been thoroughly frozen by arctic air, coating every twig and leaf with ice. Here in the Columbia River Gorge of Oregon and Washington, the Douglas firs also tell the story of strong prevailing winds from the east which dry and freeze buds on that side of trees, forcing the growth to stream downwind.

97. The dark waters of the Concord River in Massachusetts seem to disappear under the pattern of floating maple leaves. Photograph made from a bridge with 105mm lens.

103. American chestnut, once a primary forest and food tree of the entire Appalachian region, was attacked by an imported fungal blight in about 1904. Within forty years it was nearly exterminated. Throughout the eastern woods today are remnant stumps and logs,

eloquent reminders of the chestnut's size and redwoodlike rot resistance. More importantly, enough trees and sprouting roots survive to give hope to botanists that the chestnut blight someday may be defeated.

105. Interest in old-growth forests has focused on the great conifers, yet trees of all species, like this maple in a river bottom in Oregon, can grow into their own great old age. The beauty, personality, and ecological wisdom of all old trees is deep enough that it is not out of the question to "consult" the resident trees whenever human plans threaten them or their landscape.

110. Compared to the tropical forest at the southern end of the continent, the tundra creates trees and shrubs that are tiny, limited in number of species, and beset by a harsh and varied environment. Yet growth is no less exuberant, witnessed by this September day in Denali National Park and Preserve. A 200mm lens picks out ridges, one of which is shadowed by a passing cloud.

111. Oaks are among the most beloved and awesome trees of the Northern Hemisphere, and the largest ones often are not only famous in local folklore but also make connections with world mythology. They can recall the world tree, Yggdrasil, the Bodhi tree of Buddha, and the trees set to dancing by Dionysus. This pair of trees was photographed near Austin, Texas, where a recent attempt to poison the 600-year-old Charter Oak provoked a worldwide outpouring of concern and love.

112. Lying beneath a tree, one sees most clearly its interconnections to the flow of water and life and feels strongly drawn to a common center. This is a 20mm photograph of a copper beech, originally planted as a street tree but now grown to dominate a university campus in Portland, Oregon, rooted in the manicured lawn, yet wild and unrestrained above.

There is a sort of ecology inherent in photographing and assembling this book, as well. These pictures span my professional career, from 1974 into 1990. My vision of trees is rooted in knowledge gained from scientists, grows toward insights from writers and artists, and is nurtured by colleagues and friends.

I would like to thank especially Drs. Jerry Franklin, James Trappe, William Denison, Chris Maser, and Gary Hartshorn, and their students and colleagues, for views into the biology and ecology of trees and forests. I am indebted to many writers and artists for their published works, but even more to Sandy and Barry Lopez for encouragement, ideas, and the examples of their lives. Throughout my career I have found support from editors, designers, and publishers that gave me reason to continue, even during the times when they were not publishing my photographs. I would like to thank especially Bill Kemsley, Richard Hess, Chris Hill, Mel Scott, Ann Guilfoyle, Les Line, Martha Hill, Ken Margolis, Peter Howe, and Tom Kennedy. To my friends in the environmental community I give thanks for their help to me, of course, but mostly for their work for all of us and for the planet.

I am grateful for the companionship and ideas of the many friends who have been with me in the woods, shared my photographs during slide shows, and provided support both physical and moral, especially Terry Coons, Ed Cookman, Nancy and Dennis Biasi, Ellen and Bob Reynolds, Melissa Harbert, Joanna Priestley, Don Erceg, Dennis Wiancko, Brownyn and Rik Cooke, David Kelly, and my assistant Jeri Hise. I take special pleasure in remembering my trips to New England, and the friendship and support of Katy and Len Friedel, Jane and Marty Sender, and Ann Dilworth. I thank Ann, also, for advice and insights into the publishing business. Thanks to my parents, Alice and Bernard Braasch, not least, for planting the ash tree in our backyard when I was growing up in Omaha.

For the production of this book I am very grateful to Heidi and Robin Rickabaugh for believing in it for years and following through in the design; to Cindy Black and Richard Cohn of Beyond Words Publishing; to Kim Stafford for his own rich life of the trees; and to Gibbs Smith, Buckley Jeppson, and Madge Baird of Gibbs Smith, Publisher.

For love, support, ideas, patience, forbearance, energy, vision, and reasons to create a future together in a world of trees, I give thanks to my wife, Maryjo Anderson, and our son, Cedar.

Gary Braasch